Revolution of the Right

Transnational Institute Series

Forthcoming

European Security in the 1990s, edited and introduced by Dan Smith

The Korean Question: Forty Years On, by Barry Gills

Revolution of the Right

EUROPE'S NEW CONSERVATIVES

Simon Gunn

PLUTO  PRESS

with the Transnational Institute (TNI)

First published 1989 by Pluto Press
11–21 Northdown Street
London N1 9BN
in association with the Transnational Institute
Paulus Potterstraat 20
1071 DA Amsterdam

Distributed in the USA by Unwin Hyman Inc.
8 Winchester Place, Winchester
MA 01890, USA

Distributed in the Netherlands by the Transnational Institute

Typesetting: Ransom Electronic Publishing,
Woburn Sands, Bucks

Printed and bound in the UK by
Billing & Sons Ltd, Worcester

British Library Cataloguing in Publication Data

Gunn, Simon
  Revolution of the Right: Europe's New Conservatives
  1. Europe. Right-wing political movements,
  1965–1985
  I. Title
  320.94

ISBN 0–7453–0297–1
ISBN 0–7453–0306–4 Pbk

Contents

Abbreviations

CDU/CSU	*Christlich-Demokratische Union/Christlich-Soziale Union*, West Germany
DKP	*Deutsche Kommunistische Partei*, West Germany
FDP	*Freie Demokratische Partei*, West Germany
FPO	*Freiheitliche Partei Österreichs*, Austria
NPD	*Nationaldemokratische Partei Deutschlands*, West Germany
PCE	*Partido Comunista de España*, Spain
PCF	*Parti Communiste Français*, France
PCI	*Partito Comunista Italiano*, Italy
PS	*Parti Socialiste*, France
PSOE	*Partido Socialista Obrero Español*, Spain
RPR	*Rassemblement pour la République*, France
SPD	*Sozialdemokratische Partei Deutschlands*, West Germany
UDF	*Union pour la Démocratie Française*, France

Acknowledgements

Writing any book involves many people, who contribute directly or indirectly to its making. I would like to take the opportunity to thank Bronwyn Borrow, John Cayley, Ann Koch, Peter Grimsdale, John Seed and Miranda Tufnell for their support and encouragement. This work was undertaken with the financial and administrative help of the Transnational Institute, Amsterdam, and carried out under its auspices from 1987. I am especially grateful to the Fellows and associates who offered help and critical advice on the project at various stages: Mariano Aguirre, Elmar Altvater, Franco Bianchini, Stuart Hall, Basker Vashee, Howard Wachtel and Laurian Zwart. Neither they nor the Institute necessarily share the views expressed here; responsibility for errors of fact or judgement is mine alone.

Special credit is due to the editor at TNI, Sara Henley, who oversaw the production of the book and is largely responsible for such clarity of style and argument as it possesses. Finally, I would like to acknowledge my debt to Ariane van Buren, who helped plan the project from the outset, discussed it in innumerable conversations, and, above all, believed in it.

Simon Gunn
Sunderland, November 1988

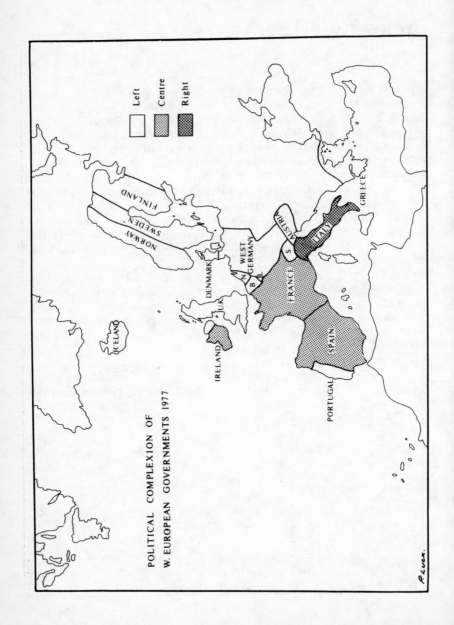

POLITICAL COMPLEXION OF
W. EUROPEAN GOVERNMENTS 1977

Left Centre Right

ICELAND

NORWAY
SWEDEN
FINLAND

DENMARK
N
WEST
GERMANY
B
L
AUSTRIA
ITALY
GREECE

IRELAND
UK
FRANCE
S

PORTUGAL
SPAIN

P. Lock.

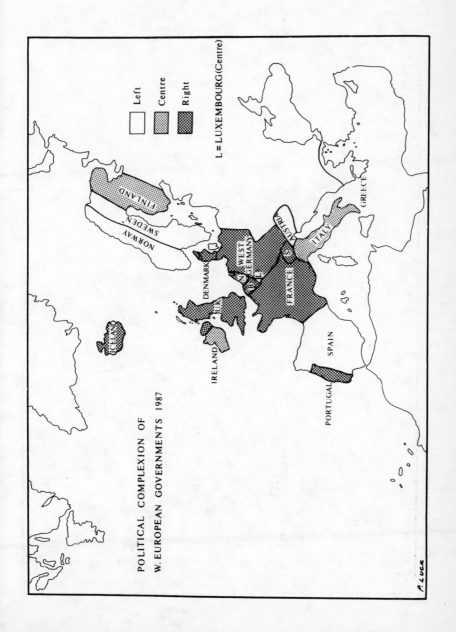

POLITICAL COMPLEXION OF
W. EUROPEAN GOVERNMENTS 1987

Left
Centre
Right

L = LUXEMBOURG(Centre)

Preface

Since the late 1970s, politics in Western society has taken a pronounced lurch to the right. Against a backdrop of global economic depression and the reordering of international capital, fundamental tenets of the post-war consensus: full employment, the mixed economy, the welfare state, have come to be questioned, rejected, and even reversed in states across the West. In a matter of years, so it seems, the age of social democracy has been rudely curtailed, and is currently being prepared for a hasty and undignified burial.

The speed with which this shift occurred caught many by surprise. Outside the narrow circle of New Right propagandists and a few critics on the left, commentators were on the whole remarkably slow to register the change of political bearings. Even where New Conservative governments were in power, they were frequently viewed as no more than a temporary deviation from the norm of post-war centrism. It was not until the mid-1980s that it began to dawn that something, politically speaking, had changed – and that it was unlikely to be undone overnight, or at the next election. The pendulum beloved of media commentators had ceased to swing.

Since then, with the spate of electoral successes of right-wing parties, the New Conservatism has been the subject of much discussion, though less analysis, in various national contexts. At the same time, the extent of its influence both in and out of government continues to be overlooked. For many, the New Conservatism begins and ends with Margaret Thatcher and Ronald Reagan. Its extensive impact on the politics of both right and left in Western states as a whole has been much less widely acknowledged.

This study does not pretend to be a comprehensive overview of the subject: I cannot hope here to do justice to the intricacy of political developments in different countries. Nor do I aim to provide an even coverage of individual states, preferring instead to forward a general argument from national examples – of which

West Germany, France, Italy, Spain and above all, Britain, form the principal reference points. If the reader notes an undue bias towards this last, then it can only be said in mitigation that Mrs Thatcher's Britain, which in compensation for imperial and economic decline has found a new role as flagship of the West European right, has not been an altogether inappropriate place from which to undertake such a study.

Briefly, this book is a preliminary attempt to apprehend the conservative forces which have come to dominate European politics, and ultimately to envisage ways in which they might be displaced by a revitalised socialism. For if the strength of current varieties of conservatism derives largely from their command at a European and international level, then it is clear that the remaking of a successful politics of the left will likewise depend on its coherence and applicability across national boundaries.

The book was written in the Spring and Summer of 1988. Even during this brief period events were altering the political map, leading some commentators to speak of the demise of the radical right and the resurgence of social democracy in the West. Their views were based largely on the electoral success of socialist parties in Italy and France. If these events did indeed signal a decisive departure from the conservative politics of the previous decade, then I should be happy to consider this book as no more than a work of political history.

Unfortunately, however, the argument that informs the study suggests this is unlikely to be the case. The political and ideological hegemony of the right in the 1980s is such as to override any local reversals: it will take more than a simple change of government, whatever its colours, to root out the pronounced anti-statism, the commitment to economic liberalism and the authoritarian tendencies that now predominate in the majority of European parties of both left and right. Establishing alternative priorities and prescriptions, and a radically different political order, will be a task for the 1990s.

Introduction:
New Wine in Old Bottles

Over the last ten years, the political map of Western Europe has been comprehensively redrawn. In 1977 the region appeared as a stronghold of Western social democracy, with left-of-centre governments in power in 12 out of 18 states. By 1987 this situation had been effectively reversed: it was now right-wing or centre-right governments that held sway in the great majority of European countries. Overall, the number of states in which left-of-centre parties had any stake in power, on their own or in coalition with the right, had more than halved. Only on the region's periphery, in Scandinavia, Greece and Spain, were there socialist governments of any description.

Even within Europe itself, this transformation has been only partly apprehended. Not surprisingly, it has been the political fortunes of the major states that have gained the lion's share of media attention. The Thatcher administration in Britain, an early and dedicated adherent to the New Conservatism, has been widely observed and projected as an international trendsetter in some quarters. Similarly, the accession to power of Chirac and the *Rassemblement pour la République* (RPR) in France in 1976, and the continued ascendancy of the Christian Democratic Union/Christian Social Union (CDU/CSU) coalition in West Germany, were recognised as significant – not only for their respective domestic politics, but also for the creation of a powerful conservative bloc in the region's northern heartlands. Much less widely heralded was the advent of right-wing governments in the smaller nation-states: Belgium, the Netherlands, Denmark, Portugal, in the course of the 1980s. Yet it is this generalised shift to the right, encompassing large and small states alike, that enables the resurgence of conservatism truly to be termed an international phenomenon.

The spread of conservatism through Western Europe has not been either politically or ideologically uniform. There are important differences in its organisation and content in individual states. These differences reflect in the first place the particular historical

1

circumstances in which parties and interest-groups of the right evolved. There is, for example, an obvious historical distinction between the predominantly secular business conservatism that developed in the north from the nineteenth century, and the Christian Democratic parties of the south, which have a Catholic, and frequently anti-liberal, inheritance.[1] The variability of conservatism is also compounded by its amorphous and pragmatic pedigree as a political ideology. Modern European conservatism has been characterised by (and indeed prided itself on) a lack of explicit theoretical principles, and a striking capacity to adapt itself to changing historical conditions.

The Historical Varieties of Conservatism

As a modern political ideology, conservatism emerged in the nineteenth century, in response to the French Revolution of 1789. From the outset, therefore, its character was defensive, intended to preserve as far as possible the old order, against the democratic principles of the Revolution. As the forces of liberalism and, subsequently, socialism, extended notions of democratic rights through the nineteenth century, so conservatism adapted itself to the task of containment, of maintaining established institutions, and of limiting the effects of mass politics on the social order.

Nineteenth-century Europe

A variety of conservative approaches to this task were evident in nineteenth-century Europe, of which three were particularly important. The first, which was most influential in the Catholic countries of southern Europe, saw society as a divinely ordained hierarchy in which each individual had a pre-assigned place. Any political change was therefore suspect, since it contravened the 'natural' God-given order, whose ideal political embodiment was to be found in the *ancien régimes* of pre-Revolutionary Europe.

The second response, articulated in its purest form by the German Romantics, attempted to counter the democratic individualism of the French Revolution by proposing as the ultimate source of political authority not 'the people', but the 'nation', as embodied in the State. This model differed from the first by abandoning the idea of God-given hierarchy and giving some credence to the fact of historical change. But it shared with it a preference for the 'natural' over the 'artificial', and a consequent respect for institutions developed over time, as against those seen as the deliberate and contrived product of human rationality. This version of conservatism found its most representative political embodiment in the Germany of Bismarck after 1871.

The third response was also the most pragmatic. It consisted of an (often reluctant) acceptance of the inevitability of democracy, but combined this with an insistence on defending individual property rights against state intervention. Political 'freedom', the right of an 'individual to do as he [sic] willed with his own', could only be guaranteed by economic 'freedom', the right of capitalist enterprise to engage in profit-making without interference from the State. In nineteenth-century Europe this brand of conservatism was developed most thoroughly in Britain, notably under Peel in the 1840s. In so developing, it necessarily moved onto the terrain staked out by liberalism, although marked differences between the two emerged as liberalism veered towards increasing interventionism in social affairs in the later nineteenth century.[2]

If this pragmatic, business conservatism was clearly distinct from the other forms of conservatism – in stressing individual property rights over deference to hierarchy or the 'nation', these latter sentiments were yet never absent from it. Indeed, in practice no single strain of conservatism I have described was wholly free from the influence of the others.

Towards a Conservative Consensus

After the First World War, the differences between these strands seemed to be diminished by a common threat: from the Soviet Union abroad, and from organised labour at home. Socialism replaced liberalism as the principal ideological challenge to mainstream conservatism. But this growing congruity proved short-lived. While a pragmatic business conservatism was perpetuated in Britain, epitomised by the pipe-smoking figure of Stanley Baldwin, the emergence of mass fascisms in Italy, Germany and Spain testified to the continued vitality of other, more virulent, brands of conservative ideology. To be sure, fascism in Germany was more than a simple extension of nineteenth-century *volkisch* nationalism, just as Franco's Spain was more than a last-ditch attempt by a landowning Catholic establishment to stop history dead in its tracks. Fascism always offered itself as a route to modernisation, not a substitute for it. Nevertheless, the ways in which European fascism continued the traditions of earlier varieties of hierarchic and nationalistic conservatism were clear.[3]

It was not until after 1945, therefore, that anything approaching an international conservative consensus could be found. This was as much a result of the defeat of, and recoil from, fascism, as of any collective redefinition of conservative principles. Historical differences remained, however. Conservative parties in Belgium, West Germany and Italy continued to bear the imprint of Catholic traditionalism, while in the Britain of the 1950s, Conservatism under Macmillan consciously sought to revive the spirit of Tory paternalism in its corporatist policies of 'industrial democracy'.[4]

Moreover, any move away from the older principles of defending private capital and upholding a hierarchic social order provoked powerful opposition on the right. As we shall see, when in the late 1940s mainstream conservative parties began to accept corporatist social democracy, an influential intellectual lobby emerged, fiercely committed to anti-state and free-market economic doctrines. Cruder forms of nationalist and reactionary sentiment continued to surface sporadically during the 1950s, in the form of race riots in Britain and *poujadist* resentment in France.[5]

As a political ideology, European conservatism has thus been marked by the variety of its forms, and their adaptability over time. Even if we discount its extreme xenophobic and fascist manifestations, conservative ideology has not lent itself to easy definition beyond the defence of property and an instinctive distrust of radical political change. Historically, it is better defined as a style of politics, rooted in sentiments of deference and respect for order and tradition, that reflect a wider desire for stability and social unity. As a consequence, it has been a style of politics that preferred to rest on implicit cultural assumptions rather than on explicit ideological principles.

The New Conservatism

On this basis it can be argued that contemporary forms of conservatism are different from their historical predecessors in at least two ways. First, the brands of New Conservatism espoused most forcefully in the United States, Britain and France have appeared deliberately 'ideological' and contestatory, and seem to draw sustenance from a more or less explicit set of politico-economic precepts. In the second place, while important national differences should not be minimised, the conservatism of the 1980s has gone a long way to override its historical characteristics in individual nation-states. Now perhaps more than ever before, conservative politicians from different countries understand each other: in a real sense they have come to speak the same political language, to inhabit the same ideological universe. For just as the social democratic politics of the 1950s and

1960s was underpinned by a shared commitment to certain political goals – welfarism, full employment, the mixed economy – across national divides, so the New Conservatism is in the process of laying down its own common agenda – popular capitalism, the minimal State, law and order – as the basis for a new international political consensus.

The ideological tendencies underpinning the New Conservatism in Western states were lucidly described by the German critical theorist Jurgen Habermas in 1983.[6] Habermas drew attention to four principal characteristics:

- the displacement of Keynesianism by explicitly demand-oriented economic policies, whose effect is to foster a society of 'ins' and 'outs', divided by access to the labour and consumer markets;
- the deliberate constriction of the functions of the State, conceived not as a 'direct dismantling of democracy, but attempts to free the State of the onerous constraints of legitimation ..., to contract the circle of themes of public debate';
- the reassertion of traditionalism in the domains of culture, education and the family, a return to a 'natural order of things', by contrast with which cultural modernity is experienced as subversive; and which serves as a counterweight to ruptures occurring in the economic sphere;
- the interlinking of the notion of an internal with an external threat, so that hostile forces from outside (the Soviet bloc, third-world revolutionaries) are assimilated to trouble-makers within a country (strikers, terrorists) and identified as analogous dangers to the security of the nation-state.

The diagnosis is instructive on several counts. It is a reminder, first, of the particular synthesis so conspicuous in contemporary conservatism: the amalgam of economic liberalism and social authoritarianism, of 'modernising' and 'traditional' elements. These components, moreover, may be seen as complementary, not contradictory. Thus the State may be conceived by New Conservatives both as an overweening presence in economic and private life *and* as a necessary instrument of social discipline through the enforcement of law and order, moral standards, and so on.

Secondly, Habermas's analysis highlights the ideological breadth and ambition of contemporary conservatism. It represents not merely a change in policy emphasis, but a comprehensive shift in the nature and direction of politics. For the aim of the New Conservatism is no less than to transform the social and economic relations of modern society. This implies that whole areas of social life not conventionally deemed 'political' are brought to the fore, as legitimate matters of public concern and policy-making. The politicisation of the 'private' is now as much an issue for sections of the right as it has long been for feminists. No politics is properly comprehensible by sole reference to the narrow sphere of government and policy-making, but the way in which subjects like the family, race and nationality have become central to the discourses of the right is none the less striking.

Finally, Habermas points out that the New Conservatism is preeminently an international phenomenon, reshaping politics in identifiably similar ways across national boundaries. The four characteristic features specified by Habermas may be most easily associated with the regimes installed in Britain and the United States, but as he indicates, they correspond to a political configuration which has been much more widely observable in France, Belgium, West Germany and elsewhere. Nor is this their full extent, for the general shift to the right has had a major impact on social democratic parties, as this study will show. The traditional left, as well as the right, has been deeply implicated in the conservative realignment of Western politics in the 1980s.

* * * *

The emergence of the New Conservatism is thus a complex and far-reaching phenomenon. What follows is an attempt to describe and define that phenomenon in its European dimensions, and to assess its likely consequences for both politics and society. The study looks briefly at the historical lineages of the New Conservatism since 1945, and how it was constructed in response to the particular political, social and economic 'crises' of the 1970s. The components of the right are then examined: its formation both within and outside political parties, the various aspects of New Conservative ideology and practice, and its appeal to identifiable constituencies. The role of parties and organisations of the left in the resurgence of conservatism, and their subsequent response to its challenge, are then reviewed. Finally, I offer a number of observations and conclusions on the prospects for the New Conservatism, its effects on European politics and society, and the task that as a result confronts the left. This task can be described, without hyperbole, as nothing short of historic.

1
The Retreat from Social Democracy

In the late 1980s the rhetoric of Western conservative leaders has taken on a distinctly prophetic tone. In June 1987 Margaret Thatcher proclaimed that socialism had been effectively abolished in Britain, and that it was now the purpose of her administration to 'set the agenda for the 21st century'.[1] The same month saw the French Minister of Finance, Edouard Balladur, describing his newly introduced privatisation programme as an historic rupture with the past:

> We are witnessing the end of an historical era, an era that believed that state intervention in every sphere and increasing taxes would guarantee progress and justice.[2]

The triumphalist note signifies more than the habitual grandiloquence of politicians. It reflects a genuine belief that the principles, prescriptions and policies which make up the New Conservatism are universally applicable, and that they are, in a fundamental sense, historically necessary.

Decline and Recovery

This self-confident right-wing renaissance is all the more surprising when seen in the light of the evolution of Western conservatism since the Second World War. For after 1945, and with the exception of Spain and Portugal, the right appeared everywhere discredited. The taint of fascism was pervasive, extending beyond parties directly identified with it, to those considered guilty by association or implication. Conservatism was held responsible for the disastrous policy of appeasement, and more generally for the failure to deal effectively with the sustained inter-war economic crisis, both of which were thought to have contributed largely to the breakdown of the international order in 1939. Conversely, the European left emerged from the war greatly strengthened, as was signalled by the landmark victory of the British Labour Party at the 1945 election, the resurgence of socialist and communist parties in

France, Italy and Greece, and the consolidation of social democracy in Scandinavia. In Austria and the Low Countries, parties of the left took their place for the first time in coalition governments.

As a result, wartime measures of state intervention in the economy and social provision, whose efficacy seemed to have been vindicated by the defeat of Nazism, were continued into the post-war years as an indispensable part of social and economic reconstruction. 'Socialism', it seemed, had become an accepted part of the political fabric of Western Europe, while across the Atlantic the progressive liberalism inherited from the Roosevelt era continued to hold sway. Writing in the immediate post-war years, the literary critic Lionel Trilling could report:

> In the US at this time, liberalism is not only the dominant but even the sole intellectual tradition. For it is the plain fact that there are no conservative or reactionary ideas in circulation.[3]

Truman and Marshall Aid

The announcement of the Truman Doctrine in 1947 and the subsequent entry onto the political stage of Joseph McCarthy were soon to provide American liberals like Trilling with a rude awakening. In Western Europe too, it was only a matter of years before conservatism began to reassert itself. Catholic-inspired Christian Democrat parties were reconstructed in West Germany, Belgium, France and Italy, and the communists ousted from power in these last three states in 1947. In the new federal republic of West Germany the election of a liberal-conservative coalition in 1949 ushered in the 20-year dominance of the centre-right. For the first time in 20 years, the socialist and communist parties in Sweden saw their combined vote fall at the 1948 elections, marking a stiffening resistance among business organisations and bourgeois parties to their programme of extending public control over the economy. In Britain, the brief flirtation with socialism was abruptly ended by the re-election of the Conservatives under Churchill in 1951. The party remained in power until 1964.

This shift in the balance of forces was the result of a number of factors, the most fundamental of which were associated with the advent of Marshall Aid and the onset of the Cold War in 1947-8. Marshall Aid was not an exercise in American altruism. It reflected a growing concern among US politicians to prevent economic deprivation from stimulating anti-capitalist sentiment in Western Europe; and to reassure American big business, fearful of economic recession at home, by restoring Europe as a market for US goods. In return, Western European governments confirmed their commitment to the basic tenets of free-market capitalism by ousting communists from office, using active repression to crush strikes where necessary (as in France and Italy) and confining nationalisation programmes to primary and service industries, such as energy and transport.[4]

It was in West Germany that the new-found zeal for private enterprise took most concrete shape: with the establishment under Ludwig Erhard, Minister for Economic Affairs, of the 'social market economy'. Based on the supposedly 'scientific' concepts of a number of neo-liberal economists, including Friedrich von Hayek, the social-market model proposed a system based on private capital and unfettered economic competition. The role of government was confined simply to safeguarding the system; any form of government control or planning was undesirable. Both the Social Democrats (SPD) and the trade unions objected strongly, but with a conservative-liberal administration backed by US interests in office, there was little that could be done.[5] By 1950, industry and agriculture in the four major recipient-states of Marshall Aid – Britain, West Germany, France and Italy – had surpassed their pre-war levels. If, for these last three at least, the 'economic miracle' was under way, then it was 'free enterprise' rather than state planning that took the credit.

Anti-Communism

The political corollary of this renewed confidence in capitalism was an increasingly vocal hostility to political forces opposed to it. Anti-communism found notable champions in the late 1940s in key politicians such as Ernest Bevin, the British Foreign Secretary, and Konrad Adenauer, the West German Chancellor, neither of whom needed prompting from the United States. Bevin prided himself on his ability to talk tough to communists, whether Soviet diplomats or members of the British trade-union movement. Middle-class radicals in the Labour Party he liked to dismiss as 'Bloomsbury Bolsheviks': in this spirit, five Labour Members of Parliament were expelled from the party between 1945 and 1950 for alleged 'fellow travelling'.[6] For his part, Adenauer was prepared to let well-known ex-Nazis like the lawyer Hans Globke, who had helped draw up the Nuremburg Race Laws of 1935, serve in his government, and he consented to the banning of the German Communist Party (DKP) in 1956.[7]

Bevin and the British Labour government, in particular, had an instrumental role in persuading the US government to take an active anti-communist stance in Europe: in 1947 they threatened to withdraw 60,000 British troops engaged in supporting the royalists' struggle against communist partisans in Greece. The result was the Truman Doctrine, whose thrust was clearly enunciated by the US Under-Secretary, Dean Acheson, in March of that year:

> Like apples in a barrel infected by one rotten one, the corruption of Greece would infect Iran and all to the East. It would also carry infection to Africa through Asia Minor and Egypt, and to Europe through Italy and France ... The Soviet Union was playing one of the greatest gambles in history at minimal cost. We and we alone were in a position to break up the play.[8]

As the Cold War intensified with the Berlin blockade of 1947–8, so anti-communism hardened and took institutional form. The Treaty of Brussels in 1948 characteristically sought to link Britain, France and the Benelux countries in closer economic, as well as military, union. It was superseded, however, by the formation of NATO in the following year. The US government was now committed to the logic of a full-scale militarisation of the region.

The result was that by 1950, 'socialism' had been undermined and conservatism revived in Western Europe, on the basis of now familiar themes: anti-communism, the preservation of free-market capitalism, and the protection of American military and strategic interests. They were themes which would continue to provide a common ideological subtext for European conservatism into the 1980s.

The Social Democratic Consensus

Nevertheless, wherever conservatism was reasserted it was forced to come to terms with the framework of social democracy that the experience of war and the programmes of the left had created. This meant accepting full employment as a priority in economic strategy, together with an extensive welfare system covering health, social security and housing. Furthermore, a substantial role for the State in economic activity had been assured by the wave of nationalisation initiatives throughout Western Europe after 1945. These various measures continued to command mass support, and successive conservative governments made no attempt to reverse them: full employment, the mixed economy and the welfare state became fixed features of the post-war social democratic consensus. By 1960, government expenditure in eleven West European states was in excess of 25 per cent of Gross National Product (GNP), and major sectors of the economy – transport, coal, electricity, central banks – were under state control in most of these.[9]

Such measures did not presage the development of socialism in any recognisable sense of the term. In no state did they denote a transformation of pre-existing social and economic relations. With the possible exceptions of Austria and Scandinavia, they were, to all intents and purposes, reforms 'from above', carried out under pressure from labour movements, but not directed by them. Significantly, the two characteristic creations of post-war 'socialism', the mixed economy and the welfare state, for which Britain served as something of a model, were designed not by socialists, but by men steeped in the traditions of Edwardian Liberalism, Lord Keynes and Sir William Beveridge.

The post-war reforms were conceived, then, not so much as a substantive transfer of power to the working class, than as part of a necessary process of social and economic reconstruction. Collectively, they were understood as providing the basis for the corporate State .and a renewed phase of capitalist modernisation. Different paths to this end were pursued in different states. Modernisation in France was characteristically guided by the state technocracy; in Germany, by the financial power of the private and state banks; in Sweden and Austria, by the institutionalised partnership of industrial management and trade unions.[10]

But if different paths to reconstruction were taken in different states, they were uniformly underpinned by a set of common political assumptions about the way in which society and economy should best be ordered. These assumptions, which came to form the basis of the social democratic consensus, have been well summarised by Mark Kesselman:

> First, an acceptance of a capitalist economy is coupled with extensive state intervention to counteract uneven development. Second, Keynesian steering mechanisms are used to achieve economic growth, high wages, price stability and full employment. Third, state policies redistribute the economic surplus in progressive ways, through welfare programs, social insurance and tax laws. And finally, the working class is organized in a majority-bent social democratic party closely linked to a powerful, centralized trade union movement.[11]

Over most of Western Europe (outside Greece and the Iberian peninsular) these prescriptions were taken as the basis for social democracy after 1950. They were also accepted, more or less intact, by the mainstream conservative parties in the West. It was this apparent political unanimity that made social democracy appear at the time to offer an end to the endemic social conflict that had plagued Western societies for a century and more. In euphoric tones, the political scientist Seymour Lipset confirmed the arrival of the new age of consensus in the late 1950s:

The fundamental political problems of the industrial revolution have been solved: the workers have achieved industrial and political citizenship; the conservatives have accepted the welfare state, and the democratic left has recognized that an increase in overall state power carries with it more dangers to freedom than solutions for economic problems.[12]

For moderate politicians and liberal academics like Lipset, all appeared for the best in the best of all possible political worlds. Social democracy was heralded as the highest stage of political development yet achieved in Western society. It seemed set fair to enjoy an ideological dominance as lengthy and unquestioned as that of liberalism itself.

Recession: the Collapse of Consensus

The history of the rise of the New Conservatism is also the history of the premature disintegration of this social democratic consensus. The economic precondition was the end of the post-war boom that had lasted from the late 1940s to the early 1970s. This was signalled by the gradual slowdown of growth-rates from the later 1960s, the oil crisis of 1973, and the onset of world capitalist recession.

A revised conservative response to this crisis was evident earliest in Britain, not least because of the singular and protracted nature of British economic decline. Between 1950 and 1973, per-capita output in Britain grew slower on average than in any Western economy. Here, between 1970 and 1974, there were intimations of what was to come in the 'Selsdon programme' of Edward Heath's Conservative administration. The Heath government aimed to tackle the now alarming and inescapable facts of economic collapse with a rapid dose of economic liberalism: dismantling the apparatus of state economic intervention, cutting back public expenditure, and reducing the powers of the trade unions. The Selsdon programme was a deliberate, if tentative, effort to break with the established norms of post-war government, to shift the balance of forces back in the direction of free-market capitalism. Although, faced with the oil crisis and the obdurate power of organised labour, it failed, this was ultimately of less importance than its role in preparing the ground for a still more ruthless and strategic attempt at enforced modernisation from the right, less than a decade later.[13]

Britain may have been exceptional in the depth of its crisis and the precociousness of the conservative response, but there were a number of common factors in the general shift to the right across Western Europe from the late 1970s. First and foremost was the economic recession, marked by two especially severe crises in 1973–4 and 1980–1, which coincided with sharp rises in oil prices. The impact of global economic depression was registered in all the West European states, though its consequences in terms of inflation, unemployment and government policies were varied. Broadly speaking, however, governments in the West – including social democrat or labour governments – pursued more conservative economic policies after 1974. These were characterised by tight monetary control, public-sector cutbacks, and a growing toleration of unemployment. But equally clearly, the failure of social democracy in many states to manage the crisis effectively, despite austerity measures, was instrumental in disorganising the labour movement and the working class, and paved the way for the conservative counter-offensive.

Conservative Counter-offensive

This counter-offensive should be understood primarily as a reaction to the labour movement's substantial political and economic advances during the 1960s and 1970s. Between 1966 and 1982, parties representing labour in Austria, Finland, France, Greece, Portugal and Spain had all gained over 50 per cent of the vote for the first time, while the German SPD and the Italian Communist Party (PCI) reached their peak levels of support in 1972 and 1976 respectively. Rates of unionisation rose, and unions themselves proved increasingly willing to use industrial muscle to achieve their ends. The number of working days lost through strikes rose during the 1970s in Britain, France, Belgium, Italy and the USA. In Britain the unions were directly or indirectly responsible for the downfall of each of the three successive administrations between 1970 and 1979.[14] In an important sense, therefore, the revitalisation of the right should be seen as a concerted attempt by employers and their representatives to claw back real gains made by workers over the previous decade and more.

The results of the forward march of labour were not unequivocal, however. The same period also saw the parliamentary parties of the left distance themselves from the new social movements: women, radical youth, greens. It was the SPD under Brandt and Schmidt that in 1972 instigated the notorious *Berufsverbot* to monitor alleged radicals and outlaw them from the civil service.[15] Likewise in the mid-1970s, the Italian Communist and British Labour parties inflicted a series of regressive and ultimately unworkable 'austerity programmes' on their own working-class bases of support.

The policies of labour and social democratic governments in the 1970s were, in fact, doubly damaging for the cause of the left in Italy, Britain, West Germany and elsewhere. For such policies not only alienated the natural constituencies of each party, but the governments themselves also became negatively identified with the climate of discord arising from confrontations with the unions, the left wing and the social movements. The memory of governmental incompetence and division in the strife-torn 1970s undoubtedly played a part in continuing to undermine the electoral credibility of social democratic parties in the 1980s.

The 'New Politics'

But there was a further dimension to this predicament. The late 1960s saw the emergence of a new range of concerns, articulated primarily, though not exclusively, by youth. These concerns, including feminism, ecology, civil rights and internationalism, constituted a major extension of what was conceived as 'political', and a redefinition of what a left politics in particular should be about.

The failure of the traditional organisations of the labour movement in Western Europe to associate themselves with the 'new politics', or to accommodate the new moral agenda, was of decisive importance. The events of 1968 were clear evidence of this. In France, Italy, West Germany and elsewhere a major social upheaval occurred outside – and only weakly aligned with – the representative bodies of the working class. A space was opened up within which parties of the right could construe the new social movements as symptoms of social breakdown: feminism came to be seen as a result of sexual 'permissiveness'; terrorism in Italy, West Germany or Northern Ireland, the inevitable product of a collapse in social discipline.

In this space the right was able in the 1970s to forge its own moral agenda: based on the family, the maintenance of law and order, and the upholding of 'traditional values'. The agenda was consciously reactionary, and intended to achieve the maximum contrast with the 'permissiveness' purportedly sanctioned by social liberalism. While parties of the right increasingly appeared to monopolise the terrain of morality, the parliamentary left could be identified with, and held responsible for, the alleged decline of social authority. In the language of a renascent conservatism, economic mismanagement and moral dereliction of duty were merely two aspects of the same all-pervasive crisis precipitated by 'socialism'.

International Capital

In fact, all governments of the period faced a set of intractable external pressures that limited their capacity to manage the crisis, in its economic dimensions above all. Among the most significant – if least observed – of these, was the deregulation of the international money-markets after the Bretton Woods agreement ended in 1973. During the decade that followed, the huge profits of the oil-producing states flooded onto world financial markets, with immediate and devastating consequences. For this new money was quite independent of, and indeed far outstripped, the value of world trade. By 1984 the flow of finance in the world economy was estimated at between $20 trillion and $50 trillion, while world trade in goods and services was put at only $2 trillion.[16]

In the absence of any international means of control for world money-markets, and as these markets themselves were becoming increasingly volatile, severe pressures grew not only on national currencies, but also on the capacity of governments to carry out strategies for economic recovery. One by one, liberal and social democratic administrations – Carter's in the USA, Callaghan's in Britain, Mitterrand's in France – were forced to forgo neo-Keynesian and expansionary policies, and submit to strict control of the money supply and public-sector borrowing. When Keynesianism, which in any case had been designed for a world of theoretically autonomous national economies, appeared incapable of providing solutions to these international problems, the bankers moved in to impose their own solutions on governments.

Still more fundamentally, the development of a supranational financial system was underscored by simultaneous shifts in the disposition of Western capitalism as a whole. The end of the long boom in the late 1960s gave rise to a phase of major capitalist restructuring, characterised by the globalisation of production and the emergence of a new international division of labour. The keynote to these shifts was the decentralisation of production: a decentralisation both geographical and organisational. Production was increasingly relocated away from sites in advanced-capitalist states, to third-world and developing countries. In Western Europe this implied a shift from the old industrial regions of the north to expanding, low-cost zones in the south: Spain, Portugal and Greece. At the same time, the control and management of production under multinational capital became increasingly complex and dispersed. The car manufacturers Ford provide a good example of the process:

> Until the late 1960s Ford UK was an integrated production network, with its own engine capacity, body plants, foundries and so on. Nowadays this is no longer so. Ford UK supplies diesel engines to Ford Europe, and imports petrol engines from Valencia. The Fiesta assembled at Dagenham used transmissions from Bordeaux, roadwheels from Genk, body panels from Spain, and suspension components from West Germany.[17]

The rapid reordering of production, typified by a growing reliance on technological information systems and elaborate methods of sub-contracting, enabled capital to restructure itself in the image of 'flexible specialisation'.

These simultaneous developments in the formation of international capitalism, which became increasingly visible in the 1970s, have had multiple implications. First, the mobility of capital as a whole has been vastly accelerated. In the words of Jeff Faux, 'multinational corporations now shift capital and locate facilities around the world as easily as they used to move them within one country.'[18] This in turn has sharpened the edge of capitalist competition, while seriously weakening the bargaining position of labour and trade unions in relation to wages, working conditions and power at the point of production. Furthermore, as national economies become ever more interlocking and interdependent, so the capacity of governments to intervene effectively for specific social or economic ends is proportionately reduced. Any attempt to pursue a programme distinct from that of other states, or independent of the logic and needs of international capital, automatically runs the risk of marginalising and bankrupting the national or local economy. As Nigel Harris put it:

> An increasingly integrated world system lays down narrower and narrower limits to the possibility of local eccentricity, including reform. In a competitive system holding down the price of labour

takes precedence over protecting it, and the domestic economy becomes increasingly a spin-off of a wider order.[19]

In short, the growing concentration and flexibility of transnational capital from the 1970s gave it greater leverage, not only over the processes of production and profit-accumulation, but also over the formulation of government policy.

* * * *

The rise of the New Conservatism was thus fundamentally predicated on the collapse of post-war social democracy in the 1970s as a viable economic, social and political order. In a number of states, notably the Netherlands, Belgium and Britain, the crisis could be termed organic, the product of long-term structural economic problems. But almost everywhere the conjuncture I have outlined – global economic recession, the assertion of labour's strength and militancy, the emergence of a supranational monetary system, and the growing decentralisation of production – served to bring the old commitments of social democracy into question. There was from the outset a clear correlation between the depth of the economic crisis in individual states and the electoral success of New Conservatives. Where unemployment rose most rapidly to over 10 per cent by 1982 – in Belgium, the Netherlands, Denmark and Britain – there also the New Conservatism was registered earliest and most forcibly.

Conversely, where unemployment levels have been conspicuously low, as in Norway, Sweden and Austria, the impact of the New Conservatism on politics appears so far to have been weakest.

Of course, the process is not one-way. As Goran Therborn observed, conservative policies to restrict the public sector and promote free-market capitalism are 'the fastest way to mass unemployment'. Thus, 'the existence or non-existence of an institutionalised commitment to full employment is the basic explanation for the differential impact of the current crisis.'[20] Yet this differentiated experience has not prevented the right from mounting a wide-ranging and widely felt challenge to the norms of social democracy since the late 1970s. Even in Sweden, for long considered the social democratic state *par excellence*, the last decade has seen an organised ideological offensive spearheaded by the employers' federation (SAF) and the right-wing Moderate Party, to revoke institutionalised commitments to full employment, the welfare state and the system of redistributive taxation. In so doing, what the right has sought to bring into question is the continued viability of the 'Swedish model' itself.

How the New Conservatism is constructed ideologically, and to what extent it has come to dominate the present politics of Western Europe, will be the subject of the rest of this book. But it is clear that the right-wing politics of the 1980s did not emerge fully fledged from nowhere in 1979. Its historical formation was intimately bound up with the post-war settlement that gave a degree of consensus to Western politics as a whole. This consensus formed around a specific set of political priorities, which were associated with what came to be known as social democracy.

It was out of the breakdown of social democracy in the 1970s, the failure of its prescriptions to deal with mounting crisis, that the New Conservatism was forged. Questions of economic management were clearly central to this crisis, but as we shall see, the demise of consensus went well beyond this: to embrace questions for long considered outside the purview of conventional politics: the role of the State in society, the family, sexuality, race, national identity. The breakdown of social democracy was also fundamentally the breakdown of a social and moral order.

The extent and depth of this displacement was recognised at the time by only a handful of perceptive observers. Ralf Dahrendorf was one of the very few to see in 1980 the depth of the engulfing crisis:

> The end of the historical strength of this [social democratic] consensus is in sight. The social democratic syndrome of values has not only ceased to promote change and new developments, but it has begun to produce its own contradictions, and it can no longer deal with them effectively ... The right-wing social democrats who administer power are sad creatures because it is so obvious they represent yesterday's world.[21]

Obvious to Dahrendorf it may have been, but it was not to the majority of the political establishment. Yet by the late 1970s the political ground was already beginning to shift, with the accession to power of a steady stream of governments of a distinct right-wing or centre-right persuasion: Britain and the USA in 1979, Belgium in 1981, the Netherlands, Denmark and West Germany in 1982. As yet there are few signs that this trend is about to be reversed on anything more than a local scale. Nor have social democratic parties, either in or out of power, remained untouched by the winds of ideological change. The retreat from social democracy since the 1970s has signalled a sea-change in the nature of Western politics, as significant in all likelihood as that which followed the final eclipse of the liberal world-order in the 1930s.

2

The Politics and Ideology of Conservatism in the 1980s

The reawakening of Western conservatism in the 1980s has been set in motion by developments at two distinct levels. On the one hand there has been a proliferation of right-wing groups, some preaching apparently novel forms of politics, others resuscitating more familiar chauvinist panaceas. Simultaneously, an ideological shift has occurred within the traditional conservative parties themselves. These two developments have been closely interrelated.

However, it would be wrong to think of the various groups and parties as collectively forming a single, seamless right. Not only are there significant ideological differences between elements on the right, but they also have different functions within the political system, and different degrees of access to political power. As a result, some groups and lines of thinking have been more central to the reshaping of conservatism than others. For this reason we should first examine the most important elements on the right separately, to assess the ideology and influence of each.

The New Right

Since the 1970s, a plethora of right-wing groups has emerged in Europe. These have been disparate in outlook and aims, yet they are frequently lumped together under the designation 'New Right'. The term is in many ways confusing: although it encompasses groups of different ideological persuasions, it is also often used interchangeably with labels like 'neo-liberal' and 'neo-conservative'. Moreover, its meaning is geographically variable: 'New Right' does not denote the same kind of politics on the European continent as it does in Britain, or the USA. For the purposes of clarity, I will distinguish between three principal groups within the European New Right: libertarian, racist and culturalist.

The Libertarian Right
Often the 'New Right' label is applied to what would be better described as the libertarian right. Broadly speaking, the libertarian

right is distinguished by a crusading commitment to free-market economics, and a concomitant hostility to the intervention of the State in the workings of economy and society – 'markets good, governments bad', as Andrew Gamble has neatly summarised it.[1] For libertarians, market forces invariably offer the most rational and desirable solutions to social and economic questions. The intercession of the State on the people's behalf in matters of economic management, education or health is not only bound to be inefficient, but it can also result in unjustifiable constraints on individual freedom.

The most widely known theorists of the new libertarianism are Robert Nozick and F.A. Hayek. Hayek is especially important as a figurehead. A former Fabian, converted to free-market economics by the experience of wartime planning and socialist advance, he became celebrated for his attack on state interventionism in his book *The Road to Serfdom*, published in 1944. In 1947 he established the *Mont Pélérin* Society in Geneva, and he helped to found the influential right-wing journal *Ordo* in the following year.[2]

The purpose of the *Mont Pélérin* Society was to bring together intellectuals and politicians united by a common aversion to the whole state-oriented direction of post-war policy. Early meetings included such luminaries as Karl Popper, the philosopher, Ludwig Erhard, Minister of Economic Affairs in West Germany, and a youthful Milton Friedman. Later conferences were attended by representatives of the British Conservative Party, Keith Joseph, Geoffrey Howe and Enoch Powell, and of the US Heritage Foundation. In the words of Milton Friedman, the importance of the society was that 'it showed us we were not alone'.[3]

This strand of right-wing politics has subsequently appeared most at home in policy institutes and 'think-tanks', which act as pressure-groups, or as advisers to conservative governments. Such bodies are now numerous and widespread: the Heritage Foundation in the USA, the Institute of Economic Affairs and the Adam Smith Institute in Britain, the Kiel Economics Institute in West Germany, and more informally, the *Club de l'Horloge* in France.

Yet it is noteworthy that even within the libertarian right there are differences of emphasis along a spectrum: from moderate neo-liberals who seek a diminished role for the State, but accept the need for a minimum level of state provision; to out-and-out libertarians who follow Nozick in viewing any type of taxation as a form of state-legitimised theft.[4] But across the neo-liberal spectrum, a thoroughgoing commitment to *laisser-faire* in the economic and social spheres is not matched by a commensurate liberalism in other areas of state activity. For both Hayek and Nozick, the State has a primary duty to uphold law and order, protect the rights of private property, and preserve national security. The commitment to liberalism is thus underpinned by a strongly coercive and potentially authoritarian thrust. These dual priorities have been evident in the institutional policies of the libertarian right. During the early 1980s, the European funding of the Heritage Foundation, which exceeded $1 million, was channelled in two main directions: to institutes active in free-market propaganda, and to organisations engaged in smearing the peace movement as 'subversive'. Significantly, it was the second of these that attracted the lion's share of the money.[5]

The Racist Right

Though it is frequently identified with the New Right, there is nothing very new about the racist right. It has a time-worn appeal to chauvinist sentiment and strong, charismatic leadership. The most publicised of racist right-wing bodies, Jean-Marie Le Pen's *Front National*, can be considered the direct heir to a long tradition of reactionary politics in France, stretching from the authoritarian nationalism of Général Boulanger in the 1880s, through the quasi-fascist *Action Française* of Charles Maurras in the 1930s, to the anti-state and anti-semitic populism of Général Poujade in the 1950s.[6] Critics like the historian Philippe Burrin have placed Le Pen and the *Front National* squarely within this tradition:

An obsession with decadence, a call to rally behind an authoritarian leader, a more or less explicit condemnation of democracy, a projection of xenophobia and racism as panaceas for the ills of modernity: so many themes which pervade, in varying doses, the annals of nationalism throughout the century.[7]

However, what is more novel about parties like the *Front National* is the combination of a virulent nationalism and racism with a strong commitment to economic neo-liberalism. Le Pen joined with other right-wing parties in France, like the *Rassemblement pour la République* (RPR), in calling for an end to the tradition of economic *dirigisme* by the State, and the creation in its place of an authentic popular capitalism. So in the 1980s, the corporatist model of the 1930s fascist state has been discarded by the racist right. Instead it has sought to identify with small business, against big corporations and bureaucratic government.

Nevertheless, the *Front National*, like other parties of the extreme right, has continued to rely for support primarily on its explicit racist appeal, bringing in other issues around this. High levels of unemployment in the 1980s have provided fertile soil for racist arguments, as is epitomised by Le Pen's curt adage: 'Two million unemployed. That's two million immigrants too many.'[8] Popular antipathy to taxation has been used to similar effect, most notably by the Progress parties in Denmark and Norway. Thus Mogens Glistrup, leader of Denmark's Progress Party and well practised at tapping the vein of racist sentiment in the electorate, rallied the party faithful in early 1988 with the assertion, 'So long as there are high taxes and Muslims, we've got something to fight for.'[9] The politics of race has been crude, but in the 1980s it has proved adept at tailoring old themes to fit new circumstances.

It has also proved electorally effective. With the exception of the *poujadists* in the French elections of 1956, no racist party since the war, or any party with a substantial racist appeal, made a significant electoral impact before the mid-1980s. The rapid rise of Le Pen's *Front National* after the 1984 Euro-elections was therefore clearly a major breakthrough: by 1986 it claimed 10 per cent of the vote and 35 seats at the French parliamentary elections; Le Pen took 14 per cent of the vote in the first round of the presidential elections of 1988.

The apparent eclipse of the *Front National* in the 1988 parliamentary contest may have been salutary, but it was due to strategic manoeuvres by Mitterrand, aided by the vagaries of the French electoral system, and not to a decline in racist feeling itself. Moreover, similar kinds of racist politics have reaped electoral dividends in other parts of Europe in the late 1980s – without attracting equivalent media attention. In Austria, Jorg Haider's Freedom Party (FPO) doubled its vote to 10 per cent at the 1986 elections, largely on the basis of nationalist attacks against the minority Slovene population in Carinthia. A year later the Progress parties in Norway and Denmark more than doubled their vote, to 9 per cent and 12 per cent respectively, by explicitly linking tax-cuts with the call for anti-immigration measures. The later 1980s have, then, seen a revival of racist politics on a scale scarcely thinkable in previous decades.

Outside these countries, it is true, the racist right has shown little electoral strength, though there are signs of a recent increase in grass-roots support for nationalist groups such as the National Democratic Party (NPD) in West Germany and the Swiss-based

National Action for People, Homeland and Vigilance. But it is in any case misleading to measure the impact of the racist right simply by counting the votes it attracts at elections. As will be shown, its influence is far more pervasive in Europe, both within and beyond party politics.

The Culturalist Right

This is the most recent, and most innovative, of the groups on the right. It emerged in the late 1970s, most powerfully in France, as a counter-thrust to the New Left of the previous decade. Indeed, many of its spokesmen in France were former members of the Maoist *Gauche Prolétarienne*. But its intellectual antecedents can be traced back more widely in Europe to the student movement of the late 1960s.

The culturalist right defines itself as a form of 'ideological action' whose object is to establish cultural hegemony in the domain of ideas, as a precondition for a New Conservative politics. So it describes its strategy as a deliberate 'Gramscisme de droite'. The culturalist right prides itself on a high-flown rejection of the political traditions of liberalism, socialism, and modern conservatism alike. Its guru is Nietzsche, not Hayek, an attachment reflected in its characteristically oppositional slogans: 'contre le totalitarianisme, contre l'égalitarianisme, contre le racisme'.

Not surprisingly, the deliberate vagueness of culturalist politics makes it difficult to identify with any coherent body of thinking. Nevertheless, certain recurrent themes emerge: a concern with hierarchy, with national identity, and above all, with cultural autonomy. Indeed, the domain of culture is the primary sphere in which political conflict is expressed: culture is the terrain on which the 'war of position' must be fought. For the culturalists it is the Coca-Cola bottle itself that represents the principal agent of imperialism, not the economic or military domination which it is more conventionally thought to symbolise.

On the European continent, it is this newer brand of politics that is most strongly identified with the New Right. Clearly, it is very different from what passes under the same name in Britain and the USA. The culturalist right is not a party or electoral grouping, but a loose federation of journals and organisations, whose purpose has been to challenge liberal orthodoxies and undermine their acceptance as 'common sense'. Its notional appeal is thus to the intelligentsia: influential sections of the professions and media, academia, and the well-educated public.

The key culturalist institution has been the Paris-based GRECE

(*Groupement de Recherches et d'Etudes pour la Civilisation Européene*) with its house-journal *Eléments*. GRECE maintains close links with groups of a similar orientation in West Germany, Italy and elsewhere in Europe. In France, the *Nouvelle Droite* came to prominence both through the extensive attention lavished upon it by the French media in the late 1970s, and through the personal connections it established with Giscardians in the *Club de l'Horloge*.[10] In Britain this movement is weak; its nearest counterpart could be said to be the *Salisbury Review* Group, with which it shares a common attachment to inegalitarianism and cultural nationalism. But the *Salisbury Review* Group lacks the radical edge and zest for explicitly theoretical confrontation that are characteristic of the culturalist right on the European continent.

Recently there have been signs, in France in particular, of a move by the culturalists towards the mainstream media. Privatisation of some channels has given them access to television; and in the former bastion of traditional French conservatism, *Le Figaro*, the thoughts of a leading spokesman Alain de Benoist on subjects such as film and video, can be found squeezed between advertisements for BMWs and luxury apartments. How far such encounters with the modern mass media will dilute the radical message of the culturalist right, or, conversely, broaden its appeal, remains to be seen.

Common Threads

It should be clear, then, that in terms of organisation, formal ideology and personnel, the libertarian, racist and culturalist rights are distinct entities. And they make little attempt to minimise their differences. With their professed cultural nationalism, the French culturalists are not averse to condemning the vulgar racism of Le Pen – though at the same time they espouse vehement anti-Americanism. Alain de Benoist, so we are told, would prefer 'to wear the cap of the Red Army than to live in Brooklyn for the rest of his days on hamburgers'.[11] Similarly, Le Pen's *Front National* and the RPR may find common ground in economic liberalism and anti-immigration policy; but differences in political style, as well as the strong mutual antipathy of the party leaders, have so far made any alliance impossible.

Nevertheless, it is noticeable that the concerns of New Right groups frequently overlap, or complement each other. For example, a similar 'anti-totalitarian' thrust, seeking to equate communism with fascism, has been advanced by both libertarians and culturalists. Indeed it is worth noting here that it currently finds endorsement in Europe not only on the German right, but also among French socialists. Racism, implicit or explicit, pervades much of New Right politics. In France the crude appeal of 'foreigners out!' is transmuted into Le Pen's carefully-rephrased slogan 'down with anti-French racism'. It finds 'respectable' intellectual validation in the concepts of 'roots', 'ethno-pluralism' and 'the right to be different' propagated by GRECE.

The impact of such ideas is always difficult to assess, but the influence of the New Right as a whole can be described as essentially ideological, rather than political in electoral or party terms. Of the three groups I have described, only the racist right engages directly in electoral politics; the libertarian and culturalist rights practise what is properly termed the politics of pressure or influence.

But this does not imply that the New Right can be considered politically marginal. It is not necessary to take at face-value the culturalists' wilder hegemonic fantasies to understand that collectively, such groups have played a part in shifting an already unstable ideological consensus towards the right. They intervene in a number of ways: through direct influence on government and public policy-making, by persistent and cumulative attacks on social democratic institutions, or by focusing attention through the media on powerful discursive themes: trade-union power, terrorism, the 'breakdown' of social order, immigration, loss of cultural identity, and so on. 'Thinking the unthinkable', the catch-phrase of the British Conservative Philosophy Group, has become a fundamental premise of the New Right more widely across Europe since the late 1970s. But the phrase has everywhere had less to do with the spirit of free intellectual inquiry, than with promoting ideological strategies designed to disrupt and transform the pre-existing political consensus.

The Traditional Party Structures

The various elements of the New Right have attracted much publicity as well as serious political inquiry in Europe, and not without justification. The impact of the New Right, especially in its racist guise, should not be underestimated: as a whole it has been instrumental in helping to set the agenda for right-wing politics in the 1980s. But the New Right itself has not been the principal vehicle for political or ideological change. In reality, its influence has always depended on developments at the political centre. The transforming impulse in European politics has come, not from the

New Right itself, but from an ideological reordering within the traditional conservative parties.

This is the most important dimension of the revival of the right. New Right ideologues and propagandists have acted as outriders for the New Conservatism by introducing ideas into public debate, preparing the ideological terrain. But the success of such ideas in penetrating party politics and government has largely depended on their being assimilated by the mainstream parties – especially the conservative parties. The New Conservatism in Europe has been shaped essentially within this context. On the whole, it has been the traditional conservative parties that have been most receptive to the ideas circulating on the New Right; they have been able to condense them ideologically, and to recast them in electorally appealing form. It is this integration of New Right ideology into the mainstream of party and public debate that has made the New Conservatism so politically powerful.

The New Conservatism that has been forged by this process is not strictly identifiable with any one of the strands of New Right ideology outlined above: libertarian, racist or culturalist. It is a hybrid, incorporating different ideas and themes from different sources, and developing them in distinctive ways, according to the political traditions of the parties involved and the different political cultures in which they act.

Broadly speaking, though, the New Conservatism in Europe is underpinned by a common dual thrust: first to modernisation, which is closely identified with the 'liberalisation' of the economy and the creation of an 'enterprise culture'; and secondly to authoritarianism, associated with a concentration of state power in selective areas and a strong emphasis on social and cultural traditionalism. In essence, there is nothing especially 'new' about either of these two components: economic liberalism and social traditionalism have played an integral part in the development of varieties of conservative ideology for a century and more. Part of the novelty of the New Conservatism lies, rather, in its deliberate rupture with the social democratic tradition of post-war politics as underwritten by right-wing parties; and in its aggressively ideological and populist style – a style often more reminiscent of demagogic leaders of the extreme right than of the remote and gentlemanly conservative politicians of the past.

But most fundamentally, what is new about the New Conservatism is its determination to translate an unwavering belief in the virtues of free-market capitalism and the sanctity of the family into social reality, to build from this new pillars of society, by

political means. It is the scope and ambition of this project – as well
as the way liberal and authoritarian elements are combined within
it – that makes the New Conservatism a distinctive phenomenon in
the political development of modern Europe.

Economic Liberalisation

The move to extend the province and agency of free-market
capitalism within and between national economies – economic
liberalisation – has been the hallmark of the New Conservatism. As
a principle of policy-making and a canon of business, it has become
all but hegemonic in Europe, where it is promulgated as an
indubitable social and economic good. Liberalisation is projected
not merely as the only sure road to economic recovery, but as a way
of increasing the sum of human freedom by extending the scope
for individual initiative and self-reliance, and expanding consumer
choice at the same time. It combines the simple theoretical logic of
nineteenth-century political economy (the 'iron laws' of supply
and demand) with the practical dictates of twentieth-century
supermarket shopping. The market is at once the agent of fantasy
and of discipline, of freedom and of restraint.

The fiscal precondition of liberalisation has characteristically
been deflation: strict control of the money supply and of
public-sector borrowing in order to reduce the rate of inflation.
Supply-side remedies to counter deflation such as lowering
taxation, abandoning currency controls, lowering interest rates,
deregulation of industry and commerce, and halting wage and price
controls are then the options available to try to encourage
investment. The effect of all of these options is to give a free rein
to money-makers. As the State's spending power recedes, those
unable to generate wealth suffer the logical consequences of
market forces.

Lower taxation, an important ingredient of the early Reaganite
strategy in the USA, has been less evident in Europe, though it has
been repeatedly promised by conservative governments in the
Netherlands and France. Even in Britain tax cuts were not finally
introduced until the 1988 budget. In Europe, strict monetarism –
tight control on the rate of growth of the money supply, which
then informs the very basis of policy-making – was probably only
pursued by the first Thatcher administration. Still, the deflationary
trend evident in Europe up to 1987 contrasts strongly with the
expansionist policies followed in the USA after 1984.[12]

Deflationary policies have thus been widely implemented by

European governments outside Scandinavia, even if they have not been promoted with the same hygienic zeal as Thatcher and Reagan showed in the early 1980s. In Portugal, under the centre-right government of Cavaco Silva, such policies saw the rate of inflation reduced from 19 per cent to 11 per cent in 1985–6, and in Italy inflation fell from 16 per cent to 4 per cent under Craxi's Socialist-Christian Democrat coalition between 1984 and 1987. Less spectacular results from the new economic orthodoxy have been obtained under the 'austerity programmes' of González in Spain and Papandreou in Greece, demonstrating that even nominally socialist governments have considered that the benefits of fiscal stringency outweighed the costs of rising unemployment, labour militancy and loss of popular support.

'Rolling Back the State'

But despite the ready identification of monetarist policies with the New Conservatism, they do not represent the most distinctive or important aspect of its economic programme. They are merely the fiscal preconditions for a more far-reaching series of policies aimed at re-ordering economic activity and social attitudes to it. The centrepiece of the project has been the attempt to diminish the agency of the State in public life, and to open up large areas of economic activity and social need to the 'free play' of market forces. To this end, a whole range of strategies has been introduced in West European states, but three in particular have been both fundamental and widely visible: the contraction of state social provision, the privatisation of publicly owned or nationalised assets, and the deregulation of most forms of industrial and financial activity.

Since the recession of the mid- to late 1970s, West European governments of all persuasions have sought to hold back or reduce public expenditure. This has meant variously introducing public-sector incomes policies, freezing social security benefits, and cutting funds for health, education and public transport. Such measures have been most vigorously pursued under conservative regimes in the Netherlands, Belgium, Britain and Denmark, but they have not been restricted to these countries. Even in Sweden, the critique of welfarism mounted by right-wing interests in the early 1980s, coupled with competitive pressures on the Swedish economy, have forced the ruling Social Democrats to speak of increasing efficiency within the existing welfare system, rather than of expanding services.

In fact, as unemployment and life-expectancy rise, nowhere in

Europe has public-sector retrenchment brought about a substantial absolute or even relative reduction in public expenditure. Even in the most cost-conscious states, the result has been a holding operation: in the Netherlands it took the Lubbers government four years after its election in 1982 simply to check the growth in government spending as a percentage of Gross Domestic Product (GDP). Thatcher's administration in Britain likewise only succeeded in reducing government spending from 43.25 per cent in 1979 to 42.75 per cent in 1987.

Nevertheless, the climate of retrenchment induced by the recession of the mid- to late 1970s has provided a cover for New Conservative ambitions to revise systematically the inheritance of post-war state provision. Thus Chirac's abortive *Loi Devaquet*, which sought to raise the qualifications and fees for university entry, should be understood not as a minor reform of the universities, but as the first step towards installing the principle of competition and 'cost-efficiency' at the heart of the French education system. Similarly, Thatcher's refusal to countenance necessary funding for the National Health Service on the grounds that society cannot afford the ever-spiralling costs of medical advance should be seen not simply as another example of governmental parsimony, but as part and parcel of a longer-term project to extend private medicine in favour of public health care in the name of competition and 'freedom of choice'.

Under cover of attacking bureaucracy and inefficiency, in a context of fiscal stringency, it has become possible to bring about a silent transformation of the post-war commitment to extending state social provision. This task is highly politically sensitive – so much so, that almost all conservative governments have been forced to retreat from it at one point or another and conduct their strategy out of public view.

By the late 1980s the lineaments of the transformation were mainly evident in Britain and France. Thatcher's aim to contract the National Health Service and state education, gradually to force large sections of the middle class and upper working class to opt for private health care and schooling, and to let state institutions become a residual service only for the poorest in society, may well in future serve as a model for other European administrations, keen to streamline state spending. In France, the narrow parliamentary majority of the right-wing coalition government and the delicacy of the issue meant that major public-sector reforms, notably of the social security system, had to be shelved. But the attempted educational reforms, and the privatisation of television stations and the prison service, all indicate that despite the tradition of administrative centralism in France the Chirac government sought to reshape state social provision along similar lines to those emerging in Britain.

The reining-back of public expenditure has thus been used by European governments for a number of purposes: most widely to reduce the rate of inflation, but also by more doctrinaire regimes to establish the principle of private virtue over public necessity in the provision of basic social services. This latter task has involved considerable political risks: in the majority of West European states the welfare system represents the most sacred political legacy of the post-war period.

Privatisation

Consequently, the most visible symbolic act to roll back the frontiers of state power has been the sale of state-held, nationalised assets. Programmes of privatisation have not been undertaken uniformly in European states since 1980, nor have they been carried out everywhere for the same political ends. Nevertheless, their implementation beyond the borders of New Conservative states like Britain and France indicates how far the right in Europe has been able to define the ideological parameters within which policy is determined.

Britain and France

In Europe, privatisation policies have been pursued most extensively by the conservative governments in Britain and France. By mid-1987, 17 major British companies, either fully or partly owned by the State, had been turned over to the private sector, including telecommunications, gas, and air travel, for a total of some $30 billion. In that year, for the first time, the proceeds from privatisation – some $8 billion – exceeded the amount raised through public borrowing. The regimen of privatisation was instituted still more impetuously in France: in a five-year programme the Chirac government planned the sale of 66 companies in which the State had a holding, and whose value was estimated at some $50 billion. By late 1987, only ten months into the programme, 23 companies, mainly in banking, insurance and telecommunications, had been privatised, bringing the State an additional revenue of some $10 billion.[13]

The scale and pace of privatisation in Britain and France made them prototypes of an apparently paradoxical process, that of a state-induced free-market capitalism. They became leaders of the trend to shift the frontiers of the public and private sectors firmly in favour of the latter. While the agenda for the welfare state remained more or less hidden, the programmes of privatisation were loudly trumpeted by the Chirac and Thatcher governments as the spearhead of their strategies for economic modernisation and the creation of a 'popular capitalism'. The Conservatives in Britain rapturously enumerated the benefits of privatisation – increased efficiency, better management, wider share ownership – and projected the whole as a form of liberation: 'letting caged birds fly', as one minister phrased it.[14] Edouard Balladur, the architect of French privatisation, was no less emphatic in his claims when he announced the programme in September 1986: 'Privatisation will take place with total openness, with the aim of creating an authentic popular capitalism in France.'[15]

Greater economic efficiency and an expanded popular stake in capitalist enterprise have been the main ideological rationales for privatisation. The Chirac government in particular has been eager to foster the idea of privatisation as a form of 'economic democracy':

> ... Our ambition was indeed greater: it was a question of involving every French person in the life of the major firms, and of thus giving employees ... the chance, by becoming shareholders, to expand the role they play in the existence and decisions of businesses.[16]

In support of such claims both administrations have pointed to the rapid rise in share ownership. According to the French government, share-owners quadrupled to more than six million in 1986–7, while across the Channel they are purported to have trebled to nine million since 1981, which encourages ministers to boast that there are now more shareholders in Britain than there are trade unionists.

Such figures are undoubtedly impressive, though nowhere do they bear out the the claims made for them by the respective conservative regimes. In business circles the Thatcher government was widely criticised for deliberately undervaluing shares in the major privatisation offers in order to achieve a wide sale; the expansion of shareholding in Britain can thus be seen as testimony to the public appetite for an obvious bargain, rather than to any deeply held belief in the virtues of popular capitalism. Again, early evidence of the emerging pattern of shareholding in recently privatised French concerns scarcely suggests a shift in the balance of corporate power. Private syndicates have easily surmounted the obstacle of the law forbidding an individual to own more than 5 per cent of the newly privatised companies. Through these syndicates, the conventional big investors – individual plutocrats like Sir James Goldsmith, the technocracy of the *grandes entreprises*, as well as the traditional petty *capitalistes à la française* whose collective financial muscle is channelled via institutions such as pension funds – can obtain a controlling stake in the newly privatised sector. Such evidence hardly bears out the French government's assertion that privatisation is commensurate with economic democracy.

Nor can it be said that privatisation automatically increases consumer choice, competitiveness and economic efficiency – in particular when an effective monopoly-holder is the subject of a sell-off. As a former head of a British nationalised industry, himself an advocate of privatisation, candidly admitted: 'The [British] government really doesn't understand capitalism. It believes that the private sector is all about maximisation of competition when in reality it's about eliminating competition.'[17] His charge was brought home by the torrent of complaints that poured down on the government about the poor service of the newly privatised British Telecom. Even the Organisation for Economic Cooperation and Development (OECD), scarcely renowned for its economic heterodoxy, has cast doubt on the gains in efficiency engendered by privatisation, arguing that 'it is government policy rather than its ownership *per se* which explains a significant part of the weaknesses of state businesses.'[18]

West Germany

Nevertheless, the trend to privatisation has been apparent in Europe even where the ideological imperatives would seem less pressing. In West Germany, the Kohl government came to power in 1983 with a commitment to reduce state holdings in the economy, but this has not been translated into a full programme of privatisation for a number of reasons. The most fundamental is the nature of the post-war German economy itself, where companies and financial institutions operate in an interlocking structure that is reinforced by generous state subsidies. As a result, many small investors prefer fixed-interest securities or managed funds over direct shareholding. In this context the potential appeal of privatisation or 'popular capitalism' appears more limited than in Britain or France.

Moreover, the existing balance of political forces has not reached a consensus on the matter. Within the government coalition, the pro-privatisation Free Democrat Party (FDP) is counterbalanced by the more traditionalist Christian Social Union (CSU) of Franz-Josef Strauss – which, for example, has come out strongly against selling the State's 80 per cent stake in Lufthansa. In addition, the privatisation lobby has to contend with the independent mercantilist policies of federal states such as Bavaria and Baden-Württemburg, which continue to give massive subsidies to major companies to ensure they maintain operations within the region.[19]

Given these constraints, it is not surprising that the progress of privatisation has been tentative; but it has none the less been gradually pushed ahead under the Finance Minister, Gerhard Stoltenberg. Since 1982 the Kohl government has reduced or eliminated state holdings in over 50 companies in energy, chemicals and transport, of a total of 500 in which it has a stake. The much-publicised sale of the State's 16 per cent holding in Volkswagen had to be postponed due to the fall in the company's stock-market valuation after the crash of October 1987. But the programme will continue with the privatisation of selected banks and, it is intended, of the most profitable parts of the Bundespost, notably the posts and telecommunication authority. Debate within government and business circles in West Germany, therefore, focuses less on the validity of privatisation, which is widely accepted, than on its scope and timing.

Spain and Italy
Indeed, it is testimony to the power of the idea of state disengagement from economic ownership and management that the ethic of privatisation has become a moving force in countries like Italy and Spain, where socialists are in government. Here state control of principal sectors of the economy was the legacy of the fascist era; and in Spain in particular, denationalisation has been projected as the economic corollary of the transition to political liberalism.

Certainly, the Spanish Economy Minister, Carlos Solchaga, has been eager to contradict claims that the socialist government is producing its own version of Thatcherite or Balladuresque strategy. So the policy of breaking up state-owned conglomerates such as the *Instituto Nacional de Industría* by selling off the more profitable concerns to the private sector is justified on supposedly non-ideological, pragmatic grounds: certain economic activities, such as car manufacture, gas and electricity, the government asserts, are 'better run in private hands'. In addition, according to Solchaga, the party has come to question 'whether the old path of nationalisation and state ownership really leads to a more just and progressive society'.[20]

The move to privatisation is less advanced in Italy, but it is following a similar pattern in the selling-off of profitable parts of giant state-owned conglomerates like the *Istituto per la Ricostruzione Industriale* (IRI) and the *Ente Nazionale Idrocarboni* (ENI). Here, the initiative to privatise has come from within the managerial ranks of the state sector rather than from the government, but again it is justified primarily on grounds of economic rationality. Thus firms like Alfa Romeo have been sold to the private sector with the idea of concentrating remaining resources in a few large-scale merged concerns, such as Telit, in order to compete with US and Japanese-owned multinationals. But if the the urge to privatisation appears to have come from such industrial chiefs as Romano Prodi, president of IRI, the coalition government of Socialists and Christian Democrats has been more than willing to support the process.

****

The desire to divest the State of a major role in key sectors of the economy, manifested in the more or less explicit sponsorship of privatisation, is, then, widely apparent in Europe. The reasons for this are complex. In part, it reflects the recognition among both conservative and social democratic European governments of the need to reorder national economies, as profound technological and organisational changes take place in advanced capitalism internationally. In Spain, Italy, Greece and Britain, it forms part of a more specific strategy to limit capital flight and attract further investment, sometimes from abroad. Hence the consistent equation of privatisation with economic modernisation and development.

But the process is also profoundly ideological. After all, under the post-war Keynesian consensus, of which the 'mixed economy' was an integral part, it was precisely the function of the State to manage periodic crises in the capitalist economy, to minimise their disruptive effects on social and economic life, and to initiate a process of controlled restructuring.

There is then something disingenuous in the claims of socialists and managers of state concerns, that privatisation represents a pragmatic or 'non-ideological' response to economic forces. Spain's Economy Minister came closer to the truth when he admitted his party's doubts about the continued validity of state ownership as

part of a socialist, or social democratic, society. For what is voiced
here is a widespread confusion about the role of the State in
modern society, about what is specifically beneficial (or socialist)
about nationalisation, and about how, if at all, economic structures
and institutions could be both democratic and efficient. It is against
the background of these fundamental uncertainties, common to
almost all social democratic parties outside Scandinavia, that the
New Conservatives have been able to implant the ethic of
privatisation, in the name of competition and economic
democracy.

Deregulation

Privatisation has been the most heralded initiative of the New
Conservative political economy, but it has in fact been only part of
a much wider thrust to economic liberalisation in Western Europe.
Since the mid-1980s, 'deregulation' has become the order of the
day. Governments have, wherever feasible, dismantled former
controls: the process has been loudly acclaimed by right-wing
journals like *The Economist* as the remedy for 'Eurosclerosis', the
'sluggish economies and wimpish politics' of the 1970s.[21]

Financial markets have been opened up to internal and foreign
competition: Paris in 1985, London and Frankfurt in 1986, at the
same time as the international stock-market boom. The average
profits of the five leading French banks increased by 52 per cent in
1986 in the wake of the liberalisation of the Bourse and the
announcement of the government's privatisation plans.[22]

Industry, and in particular labour, has been no less subject to
deregulation than finance. The Maartens government of Christian
Democrats and right-wing Liberals was among the first in Europe to
effect the de-indexation of wages; as a result, average real wages fell
in four successive years in Belgium during the early 1980s. Where
wages were formally outside state control, right-wing governments
sought to disrupt established wage-setting agreements. Soon after it
came to power in 1982, the Lubbers administration in the
Netherlands managed to bring an end to the customary bargaining
procedures that had endured between employers and trade unions
since 1945: as in Belgium, real wages fell annually for the next four
years.

Deregulation of wages has been complemented by the
dismantling of price controls: in France this policy, like
deregulation of the financial markets, was initiated by Mitterrand's
socialists in 1985, but enthusiastically endorsed by their right-wing
successors. Almost everywhere in Europe the 1980s have witnessed

the paradoxical sight of governments using legislation and state power to recreate the idyllic conditions of an unfettered market economy.

1992

The consummation of the process of European deregulation, however, is yet to come. For the European Commission is currently preparing measures designed to eliminate all remaining physical, technical and fiscal barriers to the creation of a free market throughout Western Europe in capital, goods and people, to come into effect in 1992. This plan, initiated by the former British European Commissioner Lord Cockfield, is presented as merely 'completing the European Community internal market'. But its aims are actually much more ambitious than this bureaucratic formula suggests. The New Conservatives who now dominate the European Commission insist that existing national barriers, including much domestically determined economic policy (protective and otherwise) represent a major obstacle to consumer freedom and European industrial rationalisation.

The advent of the internal market, according to its supporters, will facilitate the emergence of large, technologically advanced trans-European corporations capable of competing with American and Japanese firms. It will also serve to attract capital investment and enterprise to the poorer regions, whose comparative cost-advantages will be more widely recognised. The benefits of economic liberalisation will thus, the supporters say, be brought to all parts of Western Europe, even to regions like Scandinavia which are presently outside the EC, and which will be fully incorporated within the scheme.

But it is not difficult to discern what the real effects of such a programme are likely to be. Far from diminishing regional imbalance, it is likely to drain further resources of capital and manpower away from already declining or less developed economic regions. Not surprisingly, the representatives of countries such as Greece and Ireland have been rather less enthusiastic about the proposals than those in the 'golden triangle' of France, Britain and West Germany. They argue that the lack of existing resources in many regions of their countries may deter big investors; and that as capital is magnetically attracted to 'golden triangle' ground, the results will be akin to a form of economic 'Balkanisation', whereby the problems of the economically disadvantaged regions will be intensified.[23]

Socially, as scant employment clusters around existing centres, and labour in less developed and declining regions has to compete – by becoming cheaper – the internal market is likely to deepen existing class divisions. The model of a more or less permanently marginalised 'underclass', in, for example, parts of Britain or Spain, will thus be exported to societies where differentials of wealth have hitherto remained relatively small. Politically, it will rule out the implementation of any national economic programme that does not conform to the parameters of conservative-defined liberalisation.

So the internal market will have a major impact on European structures at almost every level. Contrary to the avowals of its champions, it is less likely to extend the virtues of economic competition and consumer choice, than to consolidate the tendency to concentrating capital in the hands of a few, which has already been accelerated by privatisation.

Still more fundamental, it represents a major attempt to achieve a political and ideological hegemony for the New Conservative political economy in Europe, to diffuse the electoral gains it has achieved in a few states like Britain and France to the region as a whole, and to make those gains permanent and irreversible. The implications for democracy of such a move are obviously very great. But that such a programme is on the agenda of so consensual an institution as the EC, and that its execution is not only probable but imminent, speaks eloquently of the extent to which the prescriptions of the New Conservatism have come to roost at the centre of decision-making processes in Europe.

The Political Agenda
Behind the diverse and often fragmentary moves to economic liberalisation, therefore, lies an ambitious project to restructure by political means the whole context within which European capitalism operates. Nor is this project as far-fetched as it may sound. Such a project is economically and politically viable to the extent that it goes with the grain of real and observable tendencies within advanced capitalism.

With the notable exception of the stock-market crash of October 1987, the New Conservatism has predominantly travelled hand-in-hand with developments in advanced capitalism. In a world economy dominated by stateless, unregulated money and large transnational corporations, it is politically convenient for governments to withdraw from any direct responsibility for ownership, management or investment in the national economy – beyond that of encouraging capital to bring about its own process of restructuring as rapidly and efficiently as possible.

Capitalism thus becomes the primary instrument of modernisation and governments can rely on its immense resources, through advertising, consumerism and material incentives, to convince the majority of the efficacy of both the process and the policies. Phrased in this way it is not an especially novel or subtle strategy. But the New Conservatism has been notably successful in asserting the essential, deep-lying symmetry of free-market capitalism, consumerism and modernity.

Behind the succession of discrete, functional economic measures instituted by New Conservative governments, then, lies a grandiose vision of an 'enterprise culture' based around the virtues of economic competition, cost-efficiency and consumer choice. Where it has been espoused most fervently, in France and Britain, the 'enterprise culture' is not envisaged as a purely economic phenomenon. It implies equally, and as a precondition of its economic viability, a transformation of what are conceived as inherited values and priorities. Thus the Chirac administration saw its programme as marking an historic shift away from a lengthy tradition of Colbertiste *dirigisme* and state-directed development. Its self-proclaimed purpose was to counteract the historical forces that had made France one of the most regulated societies in the advanced capitalist world.[24]

Similarly, Sir Keith Joseph, the chief intellectual architect of Thatcherism in its formative period, argued in 1975 that the origin of Britain's economic ills lay in the fact that it 'never had a capitalist ruling class or stable *haute bourgeoisie*', that 'capitalist or bourgeois values have never shaped thought and institutions as they have in some countries.'[25] The task of a Conservative government in Britain was thus clear: to create precisely such a class, and to establish the predominance of exactly these values.

An integral step in constructing the 'enterprise culture' is, therefore, to instal specific capitalist values at the heart of the social and cultural order. For Mrs Thatcher, 'economics is the method; the object is to change the soul.'[26] The tone is as chilling as the intention is calculated; it consists of establishing the values of initiative, thrift, self-help, competition and private ownership as the yardstick of personal and social esteem – the ethic of capitalist individualism writ large. A similar ideological ordering was promulgated just as forcefully by the Chirac administration in France. As Pierre Bourdieu observed in the aftermath of the student protests of autumn 1986: 'By extolling profit-making business ... we have arrived at a situation where the "leading edge"

– and sometimes the confrontational – *patron* has become the ideal of humanity we propose to our young people.'[27] For the more doctrinaire of Europe's New Conservatives, the enterprise culture is not simply a means to economic revival, but the agent of a whole new moral order.

The New Authoritarianism

Concepts such as the 'enterprise culture', 'economic democracy' or 'popular capitalism' are the means by which a revival of free-market entrepreneurialism is constructed ideologically. They are used to cast a beneficent glow of modernity over perennial processes of capital accumulation. As such, they are counterposed with the outdated methods of 'socialism' identified with corporate inefficiency, bureaucratic indifference and a culture of 'dependency'. But to promote liberalisation in the economy by political means may paradoxically require an increase, rather than a decline, in state intervention in economic life. As a French critic has recently observed:

> As long as the State owns the land, it directs and decides. What could be more exquisite than this liberalism which consists of increasing the power and the role of the State in the process of liberalisation.[28]

The conservative rhetoric of 'rolling back the State' can thus be misleading. Yet the apparent paradox involved is not particularly surprising or novel. It has, after all, a lengthy historical pedigree in the ideology and practice of Western liberalism; as is illustrated by the battery of legal, institutional and coercive means developed by nineteenth-century European states – and by Britain above all – to sustain the twin dogmas of free trade and *laisser-faire*. A coercive and potentially authoritarian element, then, may be present in the drive to economic liberalisation itself. Economic liberalism by no means presupposes political liberalism.

The Trade Unions

One of the clearest examples of the way state power has been used to clear the ground for a new free-market order has been in attempts to constrict the rights and activities of trade unions. The attacks originated against a background of increased industrial militancy in the 1970s. The attendant right-wing backlash sought to blame the trade-union movement for the economic crisis. This, together with the crisis itself, which brought mass unemployment to most West European states, produced a decline in union membership and bargaining power. In Britain, for example, total membership sank from 13 million to just over 9 million between 1979 and 1986, while days lost through strikes fell from 29 million to 2 million.[29]

It is in states where these conditions have come to appear endemic – Britain, Belgium, the Netherlands, and more recently France – that New Conservative governments have been able to undermine trade-union power most effectively. So far, only in Britain has this taken the form of a sustained, frontal assault. After 1982, with the Falklands War won and unemployment rising above three million, the Thatcher administration passed a succession of employment acts that reversed trade-union rights gained over the previous century.

The offensive culminated in the 1984–5 miners' strike. This was a confrontation long prepared-for by a government only too conscious of the miners' symbolic status within the labour movement, stemming from their leading role in the 1926 General Strike and their humiliation of the Conservative Heath administration in the early 1970s. The strike was notable not only for its length and bitterness, but also for the national police operation to counter it, which drew on tactics honed in Northern Ireland over a decade and more. The ultimate defeat of the miners delivered a body-blow to the British trade-union movement, from which it has as yet shown few signs of recovering. But it also demonstrated more sharply than any other event the willingness of the Thatcher government to bring the full force of the State to bear on any organised opposition to the logic of its dominant political economy.

Elsewhere in Western Europe conservative governments have proceeded more cautiously, seeking to chip away at the structure of trade-union power rather than confront it outright. The Chirac government couched its commitment to trade-union reform in the language of 'industrial democracy', of giving industries 'the liberty necessary to enhance their dynamism'.[30] The attempt to insert the principle of 'promotion by merit' in the French railway industry that lay behind the transport strike of 1986–7 was very much a test-case, involving a key group of public-sector workers. Similar, but more successful, was the strategic measure passed by the Kohl government in 1984 withdrawing the right to social security of workers laid off because of strikes by others. This was designed not merely to undermine secondary picketing, but to disorganise the

German labour movement as a whole.

In continental Europe, government action against the unions has remained relatively selective partly because the impact of recession, together with changing patterns of wage-bargaining, have as yet made more radical measures unnecessary. In Germany, Belgium and the Netherlands, the trade unions were prepared to forgo increases in real wages during the first half of the 1980s. Indeed, in some cases they were prepared to accept real wage-cuts in exchange for shorter working-hours.

Similarly, the de-indexation of wages in the Netherlands and Belgium was pushed through by right-wing governments in the wake of the breakdown of traditional methods of wage-bargaining. This breakdown has been registered unevenly, but it has been none the less widespread. Even in Sweden, for example, the powerful engineering unions' decision to seek industry-level agreements, together with the growth of independent white-collar unions, has splintered the model of centralised bargaining between employers, labour organisations and government, as it was enshrined in the Basic Agreement of 1938. Since 1984, wage-bargaining in Sweden has increasingly been conducted by employers and unions at industry level, independent of the mediation of government.[31]

But where conservatives are in power, in particular, an increasingly fragmented pattern of wage-bargaining opens up the space for governments to extract themselves from any direct responsibility for wage levels. For New Conservatives, the advantages of this conjuncture are twofold: to dissolve further the already evaporating structures of post-war corporatism, while allowing pressure from employers and market forces to whittle away the rights and bargaining power of the unions, without the direct intervention of the State.

Democracy

An authoritarian approach, using state power to constrict the rights of independent representative bodies, is not, then, always necessary in implementing economic liberalisation. But it is always present as a political option, where conditions are ripe or opposition is mobilised. Despite the rhetoric of freedom that has accompanied New Conservative governments to power, their period of rule has invariably been marked by a strongly authoritarian, centralist and anti-democratic stamp. As John Stewart has observed:

To understand the philosophy of the present [British] Conservative government it is important not to be misled by the rhetoric of rolling back the power of the State: it is a rolling back in certain sectors only. There is a further important element that emphasises the *authority* of central government. Any other source of political authority however limited and constrained is seen as a challenge to the authority. It is in this context that one must interpret the continual emphasis by the Government on the unitary State.[32]

Once again, the Thatcher administration has been seen to lead the European field in constricting political rights, whether in outlawing trade-unionism in selective areas of the civil service (General Communications Headquarters – GCHQ, in 1984), in actively denying the right of freedom of information as in the Zircon and Spycatcher affairs (1987), or in the abolition of the Labour-controlled metropolitan councils in 1986.

On the whole, the mainstream media have been slow to apprehend the authoritarian and centralising drift of modern conservatism. It is perhaps for this reason that the flagrant breaches of democratic practice that have occurred in Belgium were scarcely noted outside that country. Here a conservative coalition under Wilfrid Maartens, leader of the Flemish Christian Democrats, obtained special powers from 1982 enabling it to rule, in effect, by royal decree. The role of the Belgian parliament was thereby reduced merely to rubber-stamping a stream of legislation based on the New Conservative economic orthodoxy: de-indexing wages, lowering social security benefits, giving tax-cuts to industry, and so on. Henceforward it only became possible to challenge the increasingly dictatorial figure of Maartens through direct no-confidence motions, which the government coalition was easily able to defeat.

Institutional opposition to the Maartens regime was therefore restricted to the regional and local level. After 1985, however, the conservatives moved to establish exclusive control over the regional assemblies in the name of 'decisive' government. In Flanders a right-wing majority was assured, but in Wallonia, where socialists and Greens held the balance, illegal manoeuvring was needed to construct a majority. This involved among other tactics the forced exclusion of a Dutch-speaking representative of the *Volksunie* party, allied with the socialists, and the packing of the assembly with government supporters. The result was that the socialists, the largest party in Wallonia and the major opposition nationally, were excluded from power at every level.[33]

Given this more than questionable commitment to the conventions of liberal democracy, it was not altogether surprising that the conservative coalition in general, and Maartens's Flemish Christian Democrats in particular, suffered a severe setback at the elections of December 1987. But these events should not be dismissed as a passing anomaly. Maartens himself has been asked to stay on as caretaker premier, and there is such a delicate balance of minority parties that it is possible for a conservative coalition to return in a new form.

Neither are events in Belgium atypical. It is impossible to abstract the anti-democratic thrust of New Conservative politics in Belgium from the behaviour of similar administrations elsewhere in Europe: Chirac's government tried to push through economic measures by decree in 1986 (President Mitterrand vetoed the bid); in the same year, Craxi planned to reform the Italian constitution by introducing a directly elected president with powers to bypass the existing parliamentary system.

Racism

However, probably the most disturbing symptoms of the revival of conservative authoritarianism emerge in the powerful discourses of nationalism and race that have come to pervade the right in the 1980s. Indeed, if any *leitmotif* can be said to unite the right across Western Europe, it is a concern with these interlinking themes. Western conservative leaders like Kohl, Chirac and Thatcher may publicly seek to disavow the more forceful expressions of nationalist and racist sentiment, but both politically and ideologically, they are tied to it.

This is most clearly the case in France: here nationalism and racism are not only ingrained within the thinking of all sections of the right, old and new, but they also became an integral element of party politics with the growth of the *Front National*. As I have suggested, there are significant differences in the way issues of race and nationality are perceived and articulated on the French right. Pierre-André Taguieff has described a genuine conflict among sections of the French New Right: between anti-statist (Darwinian) and statist (eugenicist) attitudes to race. The divisions between the 'neo-liberal' conservatism of the *Club de l'Horloge* and the strong 'anti-liberalism' of GRECE, for example, are paralleled by their different approaches to the question of race. The former takes an aggressively social-Darwinian line in its emphasis on the natural 'survival of the fittest'; the latter is eugenicist, insisting on the necessity of intervention to prevent the 'dilution' of the racial stock.[34] Moreover, both these responses have been conceived in an intellectual milieu seemingly far removed from the populist racism and mass rallies of Le Pen.

But if different groups on the French right cannot be said to coalesce politically over issues of nationalism and race, the ideological similarities are none the less marked. Both the *Front National* and the *Club de l'Horloge* are open in their admiration of the strong leader; like GRECE, they base their politics on the supposed decadence of French society, its social, cultural and moral degeneration, which is summed up in the single word, *laxisme*. Against this is posited not only the notion of order and hierarchy, but more profoundly of *enracinement* or 'rootedness', a central concept in French right-wing thought that goes back to Maurras, the quasi-fascist *Action Française* in the 1930s, and beyond. The ideological functions of *enracinement* are multiple: it conflates biological and cultural forms of racism in defining 'national identity', it marks off 'alien' communities and cultures, and it berates the left for its alleged lack of patriotism.

Given this ideological context, as well as the steady electoral advance of Le Pen and the *Front National* in the mid-1980s, it was almost inevitable that the traditional conservative parties in France, the RPR and the *Union Démocratique Française* (UDF), would themselves shift to the right on such issues. In fact, when they were in opposition after 1981, prior to the rise of Le Pen, the RPR and UDF had already developed their own racist programme, including the notorious scheme of 'national preference' whereby those with French citizenship would deliberately be favoured over immigrant workers in, for example, the receipt of state benefits. This policy was toned down after 1985 under pressure from church interests, only to be taken up and expanded by the *Front National*. But on coming to power the Chirac administration did not seek to jettison the rest of the RPR/UDF proposals – to widen the powers of the police to harass 'aliens', to restrict immigration from non-EC countries, and to extend the grounds for expulsion. By April 1988 Chirac could boast as part of his presidential bid that under his government 130,000 'illegal aliens' had been deported.[35]

The effect of rising support for Le Pen on the traditional centre-right parties between 1986 and 1988 was in fact two-way. On the one hand, it exacerbated divisions between Barre's UDF and Chirac's RPR, and within the RPR itself. While some, like the Interior Minister Charles Pasqua, argued that the coalition should maintain a strong nationalist image to attract the *Front National* vote, others, such as Michel Noir, Minister for Foreign Trade, and Michèle Barzach, Minister of Health, opposed such moves to the point of threatening to resign. The effect of their opposition, as well as that of President Mitterrand and wider sections of French public opinion, was to sensitise issues of race, and forestall further repressive measures which the right of the RPR wished to see implemented.

On the other hand, the demands of electoral *realpolitik* forced the administration to affirm a hard line on questions of race and immigration, in order to appeal to Le Pen's supporters while maintaining a respectable distance between the RPR/UDF coalition and the *Front National*. These pressures did not always come from outside the parties of the centre-right: a poll in 1987 showed that a third of RPR members considered Le Pen a natural ally.[36] But the presence of the *Front National*, and the perceived need to appeal to its swelling constituency, were undoubtedly of major importance in sustaining race as a central political issue on the 'respectable' right. Thus Chirac responded to Le Pen's advance in the first round of the 1988 presidential elections with the promise 'to preserve our national identity and to combat illegal immigration', while even the less enthusiastic Barre called for a 'common European frontier against new immigrants'.[37] The phrasing may be more restrained, but it was the radical right that had succeeded in setting the terms of debate.

It is in France that nationalist and racist sentiments have found their most powerful political expression; not least through the combined activities of an intellectual right, which set the discursive agenda, and the *Front National*, which gave it mass appeal. To some extent developments in France have served as a model, both of the effective mobilisation of a racist right and of the ambiguous relationship of traditional conservative parties to it.

This ambiguity has long been evident in the attitudes of the British Conservative Party. Despite Le Pen's stated admiration for Thatcher and her policies, he was not permitted to speak at the 1987 Conservative Party conference. Yet, as Sir Alfred Sherman, Thatcher's former close adviser who issued the invitation, pointed out, Le Pen's 'views on wider share ownership, foreign affairs, the family, law and order and education might well ring sympathetic chords with a substantial number of British people, particularly Conservatives'.[38] The same apparent ambiguity was evident in a celebrated television interview by Thatcher in 1979, when she condemned the British National Front only to assert that the country was in danger of being 'swamped by an alien culture'.[39]

The significance of such ambiguities, as Gill Seidel has observed, lies less in the existence of formal organisational connections between conservative parties and racist groups, than in the 'discursive continuities and overlaps' which link them and serve to construct a wider 'common sense' on issues of nationality and race.[40] The most potent intervention in Britain – one to which the Conservative Party has largely contributed – has been on the question of anti-racism. Focused particularly on Labour-led education and local government policies, and orchestrated by members of the *Salisbury Review* Group with government complicity, the purpose of the intervention has been to transmute racism from a political and institutional issue into a purely moral and individual one. By promoting anti-racist policies, so the argument goes, such groups are heightening, rather than diminishing, racism – by highlighting racial differences and stirring racial tension.

Behind these arguments, however, lies the assumption not merely that social and institutional racism are figments of the left's imagination, but also that national and racial allegiances are natural, inevitable and even desirable, and should not be obstructed. And this, in turn, is used to validate the notion of a dominant, immutable 'national culture', transmitted through such diverse media as education and the heritage industry, and which represents the expressive essence of 'Englishness' – or as Seidel puts it: '"we" have culture, "they" have ethnicity.'[41]

Many of these arguments of the British right clearly approximate to the slogans of their French counterparts: 'à bas le racisme anti-français' or 'défendre les français'. But even where racism and nationalism are more problematic political themes for conservatives, as in West Germany, there are echoes of a similar discourse. Thus it is possible for Franz-Jozef Strauss to talk of the need for German society to overcome its historical guilt complex, to 'move out of the shadow of the Third Reich', and to attack the left for its evasiveness and ambivalence on questions of German nationalism.[42] During the 1987 election campaign both the Christian Democratic Union (CDU) and the Christian Social Union (CSU) deliberately set out to rehabilitate traditional conservative values through the notion of *Heimat* – 'homeland' – identified with the 'middle Germany' of small towns and rural villages.

Yet there is, as always, a less sentimental obverse to this moderate German nationalism, as for example in the tightening of checks on foreign workers' permits, and the repatriation schemes introduced by the Kohl government. Immigration briefly became an open issue in the 1983 election, when Kohl threatened to change the constitution to stem the influx of unwelcome refugees through East Berlin. It remains a barely acknowledged but persistent subtext of German politics.

Traditionalism

Nationalism in general, and racism in particular, represent the pervasive and invariably ugly faces of conservative authoritarianism in Europe. They are not, however, isolated or discrete tendencies within right-wing ideology, but are inserted in multiple ways into a broader assertion of social and cultural 'traditionalism'. In the perception of a 'breakdown of law and order', for instance, which has been an obsessive theme of New Conservative ideology from Thatcher and Kohl to Le Pen, it is invariably immigrant communities that are implicated in the rising incidence of crimes such as 'mugging'.[43] Equally, in debates on the family in Britain and the USA, New Conservative critics have lighted upon the supposedly 'unstable' structure of *black* families as a major cause of past policy 'failures'.[44] Racism of a peculiarly insidious kind has thus become woven into the fabric of New Right responses across the range of social issues, from education to poverty and welfarism.

Yet 'traditionalism', defined as the attempt to restore a 'natural' moral order in the face of changes in social legislation and behaviour since the 1960s, is itself closely linked with the authoritarian thrust of the New Conservatism. This is evident, for instance, in the renewed emphasis placed by conservatives like Thatcher and Reagan on the family as the fulcrum of conservative social policy. For this restitution of the 'traditional' family is, as Leonore Davidoff and Catherine Hall have observed, a concerted attempt to install at the centre of social relations a model 'constructed on a specific type of family authority and sexual division of labour', independent of secular trends in social and sexual behaviour, and often at the expense of those who do not conform to it.[45]

In effect, what the conservative revival of the family is concerned to reassert above all is a 'traditional' (nineteenth-century) definition of gender differentiation: to reaffirm, in the words of a recent New Right commentary, 'the dignity of the dual roles of men and women'.[46] At one end, this can lead to a kind of pseudo-mystical psychologising, which appears superficially to borrow its language from the women's movement: 'Women have long horizons within their bodies, glimpses of eternity sited in their wombs.'[47] At the other, and far more decisive end, it demands that men reassert their role as principle breadwinner and household head while women are forced out of the labour market and back into the home. Much of the debate in the late 1970s and early 1980s on unemployment and its remedies could be seen to circle round this theme: a theme in which, incidentally, the trade unions and much of the left were not infrequently complicit.

New Conservative social policy has in fact already taken significant legislative steps to fulfil this aim: reducing maternity and child benefits, removing day-care services and so on, in conservative states across Western Europe. However, in the context of economic liberalisation and the 'freeing up' of both capital and labour markets, this traditionalist emphasis in the social sphere spawns a number of potentially awkward inconsistencies for conservative policy-makers. Thus Lord Young's proposals for deregulation in the European Community in anticipation of the 1992 European internal market simultaneously oppose the extension of equal-employment rights for married women across national frontiers.[48] The universal logic of the market only applies, it would seem, where men are concerned.

Such policies have already had a substantive effect on the economic position of women. Not only have they reinforced, along with developments in the international economy, existing wage differentials between men and women, or pushed women out of the labour market altogether; but also they have served to foster the process that has been termed the 'feminisation of poverty'. Barbara Ehrenreich noted of the USA that 'in 1980 two out of three adults who fit the federal definition of poverty are women', a proportion which expanded further under the impact of the Reagan programme.[49] Equally in Britain, conservative social policies have aggravated a long-term trend towards increasing female poverty. As Peter Townsend noted in 1984:

> Between 1971 and 1981 the numbers of one-parent families increased by 71 per cent and now stand at nearly one million families ... The long-standing inequality between the sexes in access to resources and the institutional bias in favour of conventionally married couples contribute to the poverty which lone parents and their children experience.[50]

Since the vast majority (about 90 per cent) of single parents are women, and the 'inequality' and 'institutional bias' Townsend mentions have been intensified by conservative social policy, it is not difficult to apprehend that the same 'feminisation of poverty' described by Ehrenreich in the USA is likewise inevitably occurring in Britain and the conservative-dominated states of continental Europe.

It should be emphasised that the idealised conception of the 'traditional' family, on which so much of conservative social policy rests, cannot be said to correspond with any observable social reality. The proportion of families in Britain that conform to a classical nuclear model (father 'at work', mother 'at home', two children) is currently a mere 5 per cent.[51] Nor are there firm grounds for assuming that the institutions of marriage and the family are under threat, as conservative propagandists have argued. While in almost all West European societies marriage has never been more popular, judging from statistical evidence, divorce rates have also risen rapidly, suggesting that marriage by no means necessarily brings with it stability.[52]

Furthermore, the growing professional and media attention given to the prevalence of domestic violence and sexual abuse now evident across Western Europe questions, at the very least, the myth of the home as the preserve of secure and harmonious relations. For while such cases have predictably been used by sections of the media and the right to attack the social services for 'inventing' problems and 'meddling' with the rights of parents, what they suggest more profoundly, as recent critics have pointed out, is that something may be wrong in 'normal' as well as in 'peculiar' families.[53]

Nevertheless, an idealised conception of the family acts as the ideological pivot around which a much more extensive moral agenda can be activated. It serves as a prop, for example, to the anti-abortion lobby – even if many conservatives do not in practice support this. It is used even more vociferously as a means of asserting norms of sexual behaviour. Thus the notorious Clause 28 of the 1988 Education Bill introduced by the British Conservative government forbids, among other things, the promotion of homosexuality by local councils as 'a pretended family relationship'. Similarly, Le Pen's repeated attacks on homosexual men, playing on fears of Aids and calling for the isolation of victims, needs to be related to his simultaneous denunciation of *laxisme* and his call for a return to 'traditional family values'. In the hands of the New Conservatives, the slogan of the women's and gay liberation movements, 'the personal is political', has been turned against its protagonists in order deliberately to constrict the range of legitimate social identities or modes of behaviour.

This inversion is in fact characteristic of the way in which the

New Conservatism has demonised the 1960s and the liberal reforms associated with it (many of which were in fact passed in the early 1970s). The British Conservatives have once again led the way in Europe, with their excoriation of the 'permissive society' and their insistent demand for a moral revival based around traditional (or 'Victorian') values. Indeed, Thatcher has repeatedly affirmed that the primary task in her third term is personally to instigate a moral renaissance to complement the triumphant establishment of the enterprise culture.

Neither have conservatives elsewhere been slow to blame present or recent ills on the political and cultural ferment of the 1960s. The German right, for example, has glibly sought to hold the group of critical theorists known as the Frankfurt School, which was popular in the 1960s among student radicals, responsible for the subsequent terrorist violence of the Red Army Faction.[54] What such accusations reveal is at once a profound anti-intellectualism and a deep-seated intolerance on the right for the idea that German society might be otherwise ordered.

But closer inspection suggests that sections of the European right have actively adopted – and subverted – arguments and strategies previously associated with the socialism and libertarianism of the 'permissive moment'. This is most evident in France, where the culturalist right in particular, whose own roots lie in 1968, has taken an almost perverse delight in appropriating the issues and inverting the techniques of the former New Left: anti-imperialism on behalf of European and third-world nationalisms, anti-bureaucracy identified above all with the socialist State, and so on. Even Le Pen's denunciation of the 'system', which he associates with the existing state apparatus as well as the established political parties, and his celebration of 'direct democracy' can be seen to draw on aspects of the language and critiques of 1968. Likewise in Britain the Thatcher government has skilfully presented its educational reform, the thrust of which is both authoritarian in its pedagogic prescriptions and centralising in administrative effect, as an extension of 'parent power', a blow on behalf of popular control against the overweening State.

A Potent Cocktail

In short, the European right has frequently proved remarkably eclectic and strategic in its orchestration of political themes. This does not simply mean that it has engaged in ideological manipulation in order to engender a mass 'false consciousness'.

Parties of the right have tapped into real concerns and anxieties among their respective electorates – the unresponsiveness of bureaucracy, safety on the streets, the need for collective (national) identity and so on – which the left has all too often shied away from. As Taguieff notes in his analysis of the *Front National*:

> the mainstream parties have all, and always, avoided confronting what are perceived, rightly or wrongly, as 'problems' of everyday life: immigration, the Maghreb issue, unemployment, insecurity – themes that people live with an intensity that brings the propaganda of the *Front National* sharply into relief, and which invite comparison – hence an ideological payoff for its leader ...[55]

Similarly in West Germany, it is the right-wing parties that have capitalised on popular antipathy to the burgeoning bureaucracy associated with two decades of a social democratic government's calls for 'human administration'. And again, it is the CDU and CSU that have succeeded in monopolising the language and values of *Heimat*: ideological ground which the German left, including the Social Democrats (SPD), vacated long ago because of its historical resonances.

Indeed, what is characteristic of the new ideologies of the right is the manner in which supposedly non-political issues – the family, personal morality, nationality – are actively incorporated and harnessed in political discourse. It is this dimension that not only gives the far right its claim to 'frank-speaking', but that also serves as a vehicle for transmitting New Conservative policies to electorates. As Stuart Hall has observed, none of Thatcher's major measures, from privatisation to educational reform, has been advanced without first being constructed ideologically through concepts like the 'share-owning democracy' or 'parent power'.[56]

Equally significant is the way in which the New Conservatism has linked themes, whether 'traditionalist', 'authoritarian' or 'libertarian' in emphasis, and moulded them into a coherent political ideology. Thus, 'featherbedded' trade unions are linked not only to the 'non-competing economy', but also to the 'nanny State' which, in turn, is held responsible for fuelling unrealistic (because 'unearned') expectations, which carry inescapable consequences: the breakdown of social discipline, the weakening of parental authority, rising crime rates, and so on.

It is this capacity to transmute politics into the realm of the 'non-political', the everyday, and at the same time to weld diverse ideological elements into a cohesive political 'common sense' that has become both the trademark of the new forms of conservatism and an important reason for their appeal. Invariably, the new comes draped in the language of the commonplace. Thus Margaret Thatcher enunciated her political creed in terms of a banalised tradition:

> My policies are based not on some economic theory but on things I and millions like me were brought up with. An honest day's pay; live within your means; put by a nest egg for a rainy day; pay your bills on time; support the police.[57]

So the conservatism now prevalent in Western Europe is capable of condensing diverse themes: the 'traditional' sits alongside the innovative or 'modernising'. This is a major part of the political project. Indeed, it can be argued that this amalgam of modernising and traditional elements has become the distinguishing feature of West European politics in the 1980s, though the complexities of coalition governments and differing party systems can often conceal it.

Only in Britain, of the larger European states, are the two ideological elements successfully fused in a single party. Elsewhere, they are provided for by different parties operating as partners within a coalition. In West Germany, for example, the neo-liberalism of the FDP and the authoritarian traditionalism of Strauss's CSU reinforce similar existing, though milder strands within the dominant CDU. In Belgium between 1981 and 1987 government was shared between an economically neo-Thatcherite Liberal Party and Maartens's strongly traditionalist Flemish Christian Democrat Party.

But a similar ideological composite may be found even in states where parties of the traditional left have a stake in power. In Italy, Donald Sassoon has suggested, it has been Craxi's Socialists who – having jettisoned ideas of a socialism associated with the welfare state or based on the working class – are now identified with a modernisation shorn to its economic essentials and without the encumbrance of concomitant social reforms. The traditionalist ballast in the coalition has been provided by the majority Christian Democrats, who since 1983 have returned to their customary emphasis on the twin pillars of Church and family. 'Together they define all that is "possible". There is no alternative.'[58]

Clearly, the New Conservatism has been highly successful in welding an effective political ideology from diverse and outwardly contradictory elements, and in developing it as a viable form of mass politics. This has involved a strategic appeal not only to traditional sources of support for the right, but equally to new sources of support from increasingly fluid and socially heterogeneous electorates. Whether the 1980s have witnessed the demise of class politics in Western Europe is debatable to say the least, but there is little doubt that the right has proved itself more capable than the parties of the left of capitalising politically on changes in social and ideological formation.

This does not automatically imply that societies and electorates have themselves somehow become innately conservative: the right has again understood better than the left that parties do not passively reflect a reservoir of pre-existing attitudes, but instead play an active part in shaping those attitudes politically. Parties fashion constituencies for particular forms of politics. In order to see more clearly how this has been achieved, we need to examine briefly the social bases of support for parties of the right, and the sources of their appeal.

3

The Constituencies and Appeal of Conservatism

The social basis and appeal of the newer forms of conservatism in Western Europe have not received much systematic attention. Political philosophers have concentrated on the novel theories expounded on the right. Political scientists have been preoccupied with the decline of the traditional mass parties of the working class and the rise of the new 'single-issue' parties, like the Greens.

As a result, we have a sketchy understanding of precisely why and to whom the New Conservatism appeals. The serious explanations that have been forwarded tend at one extreme to be restricted to interpretations of voting behaviour, which is seen as revolving around a conventional parliamentary 'left-right' axis, without reference to the deeper ideological shifts that underpin changes in support for parties. Or, at the other extreme, answers have been sought in the realm of 'post-materialist' values, in the transition from a politics concerned with basic economic and class interests to one centred around questions of lifestyle and consumption.[1]

The capacity of either of these approaches to explain political change is limited. What is absent in both is a critical attempt to understand how the right has capitalised on the complex social and ideological movements in Western societies. The right has tried not simply to reflect changing attitudes, but to create new constituencies out of shifting social formations.

Voting Patterns

Analysing these tendencies is far from simple. Voting preferences, for example, do not automatically mean support for a particular political philosophy. Likewise, opinion polls do not disclose the existence of a rational or consistent set of political attitudes among populations or social groups. It is also difficult to know which constituencies to evaluate. In many West European states, as we have already seen, the New Conservatism is identifiable not with any single party, but with the combined politics of different parties in a broad coalition. So it is necessary to speak of a number of distinct constituencies for aspects of the New Conservatism, rather than of any homogeneous bloc of support.

The Middle Class

Historically, conservatism has been heavily identified with the upper and middle classes – land and business united in common defence of property. These groups, flanked by higher professionals and civil servants, remain the most solid supporters of conservative parties throughout Europe.[2] In both the British and West German elections of 1983, 60 per cent of the 'middle class' voted for the Conservative or Christian Democratic and Christian Social Union (CDU/CSU) parties respectively, and commensurate or higher figures can be found in most West European states.[3] Moreover, as parties of and for the middle class, they tend to attract the votes of a higher proportion of that class than do the equivalent representative parties of the working class. Only 36 per cent of manual workers in Britain, and 51 per cent in West Germany, voted for the Labour Party and Social Democratic Party (SPD) respectively in 1983.[4]

However, this does not mean that the middle and upper classes can be viewed as a uniform political bloc. In the first place, the middle-class vote may be spread across different parties of the right. In France, for example, extreme-right parties have long found support among ultra-conservative sections of the Catholic bourgeoisie, and the tradition is continued in backing for Le Pen and the *Front National*. Similarly, in West Germany the Free Democrat Party (FDP) has customarily drawn the bulk of its votes from white-collar workers and civil servants, while the CDU/CSU has attracted the core groups of an older middle class: business, the established professions, farmers, etc. As long as these parties are in coalition, as has been the case in Belgium and West Germany for most of the 1980s, the middle-class identification with conservatism is more or less solid.

The 'New Middle Class'

One key feature is that the 'new middle class' of salaried and technical workers, whose political nature is characteristically amorphous, has become increasingly linked to the right. This trend represents the first tangible factor in the electoral success of the New Conservatism. In most West European states, this new middle class emerged as a distinct social entity in the late nineteenth and early twentieth centuries. Politically it tended to be conservative, seeking to distance itself from the skilled working class, and to approach the lifestyle and values of the established professional and commercial middle class.[5]

However, there was nothing permanent or inevitable in the attachment of the new middle class to the political right. Its existence was not tied inextricably to the profits of private capital. After 1945 the group expanded rapidly in both numbers and importance, with the extension of state provision and the creation of a large public sector. Henceforward its interests appeared to be more closely bound to the expansion of the public sector rather than to the profitability of private capital. Political identification consequently tended to shift away from the right to parties of the left, which was most directly associated with the growth of the public sector and state employment. At the same time the expansion of this group, which included teachers, clerical staff, technicians and health workers, greatly enhanced its electoral significance. During the 1960s and early 1970s the dominance of the social democratic left in states like West Germany, Britain, Denmark and, later, France was based largely on the capacity of their respective moderate left parties to attract the vote of the new middle class and professionals.

But since the mid-1970s the new middle-class vote has moved steadily to the right – although not necessarily or immediately to the conservative parties. The reasons for this class's disillusionment with social democratic parties lie largely with the performance of those parties in government during the 1970s: their public-sector job-cuts, the way they held down wages and salaries, the rise in the rate of inflation, and so on.

Further, since 1980 social democratic parties have not managed to win back the support of this group. After its electoral failure in 1983, the German SPD based much of its hope for the 1987 election on recapturing the votes of the 'technical intelligentsia'. In fact its decline among new middle-class voters merely continued, falling from 50 per cent to 43 per cent between 1980 and 1983, and down again to only 37 per cent in 1987. The main beneficiaries were the right-wing CDU/CSU coalition, whose vote rose by 10 per cent among this group between 1980 and 1987, the Greens (up 8 per cent) and, to a lesser extent, the FDP, who gained an extra 2 per cent between 1983 and 1987.[6] Similarly, in both the 1983 and 1987 elections the British Conservative Party managed to obtain over half the white-collar vote, against only 20-21 per cent for Labour.[7] It appears that in these states, at least, substantial sections of the new middle class have fallen back on old loyalties, and now feel that their interests are tied to the expansion of private capital, rather than to the growth of the public sector.

On the other hand, in states where social democratic parties are the ones to have provided the modernising force in the drive to economic liberalisation in the 1980s, important sections of the middle class have been quite prepared to switch traditional allegiances and lend support. Polls published prior to the 1987 Italian election, for example, showed that the majority of businessmen and managers, as well as professionals and white-collar workers, preferred the Socialist Craxi as Prime Minister over his Christian Democrat rival, De Mita.[8] Likewise, the tough 'neo-liberal' programme of the Portuguese Social Democrats (SD) enabled them to persuade the great bulk of the middle class to abandon the traditional parties of the right, boosting the SD vote by an astonishing 20 per cent between 1985 and 1987.[9] It seems clear that the New Conservative politics have extensive appeal across the middle classes – most especially where economic liberalisation is seen to be counterbalanced by an emphasis on social traditionalism, as in Britain, Italy, West Germany, Portugal and France.

Divisions within the Middle Class

But not all sections of the middle class are equally implicated in the shift to the New Conservatism. Much has been made of the divisions recently apparent within the middle class, based on factors such as access to higher education. Commentators have highlighted the comparative lack of enthusiasm for conservatism among university-educated voters in states like Britain and West Germany, in contrast with those in the middle class who had other forms of vocational training.[10] In Britain, for example, the Conservative vote among university graduates diminished by 9 per cent between 1983 and 1987, accounting for only 34 per cent of the group at the later date; a survey in 1988 likewise showed graduates to be far more distrustful of the activities and regulation of the City of London than the population at large.[11] In states like Denmark, Norway and Britain, conservative policies have also been markedly less popular among middle-class public-sector employees than with their counterparts in the private sector.

Though these trends seem clear enough, their significance is not entirely obvious. First, these political divisions within the middle class do not seem uniform across Western Europe. Outside Britain and West Germany, for instance, graduates have been as likely to support parties of the right as of the left. Second, they do not correspond to any permanent structural divisions, so their longer-term political effects are unclear. Finally, their electoral consequences in both Britain and West Germany were less to strengthen the traditional mass parties of the left, than to augment the centre or marginal parties: the Liberal/Social Democratic (SDP) Alliance and the Greens. As far as voting goes, such divisions do not substantively diminish the political dominance of the New Conservatism, or its hold over the broader middle class. They merely provide exceptions to the general rule.

The Working Class
The return to the conservative fold of the middle classes is one thing: but much the most widely noted electoral feature of the New Conservatism has been its capacity to attract the votes of manual workers – especially the skilled – who were formerly the electoral mainstay of the social democratic parties. From their inception in the late nineteenth and early twentieth centuries in Europe, such parties based their organisation and appeal on the working class. Although after 1945 their constituencies widened, the interests of the working class remained in theory at the heart of social democratic politics.

During the 1960s and 1970s, however, parties of the left became increasingly distanced from their working-class bases of support. The switch to the right among large numbers of working-class voters in the late 1970s and early 1980s was clearly significant. It reflected, in many cases, a desire among workers to break free of the shackles of pay restraint that had been imposed by social democratic governments and to return to conditions of free collective bargaining. But it was also a protest against parties of labour, which appeared increasingly incapable either of solving the prolonged economic crisis, or of initiating major social reforms.[12] The New Conservatism seemed to offer the prospect of both substantial material incentives for skilled workers, and a radical break with the ossified structures of social democracy.

The trend was first amply demonstrated in the British election of 1979, when the Conservatives swept to power on the back of an 18 per cent swing among skilled manual workers.[13] In the two elections that followed, this identification has been sustained: more skilled workers (40 per cent) voted for the Conservatives than for any other party.

The same swing was visible elsewhere after 1980: in West Germany in 1983, when 44 per cent of manual workers voted for the CDU/CSU; and in France in 1986, when the vote for the parties of the right was swelled by working-class defectors from the Socialist and Communist ranks.[14] Likewise in Italy, the 1987 elections saw the continued decline of the Communist Party, the traditional vehicle of the working class, which suffered a widespread loss of support in former strongholds such as the northern industrial belt.[15] The rupture of working-class identification with the historical parties of labour, compounded if not initiated by the New Conservatism, appears almost universal outside Scandinavia and Austria.[16]

However, the pattern is in fact more differentiated than these figures might suggest. In contrast to the skilled working class, semi- and unskilled workers remain the social groups most strongly resistant to the appeal of the New Conservatism. Indeed their resistance has hardened during the 1980s in Britain, France and West Germany. Where the cultural and institutional framework of a working-class community persists, this resistance is particularly reinforced: trade unionists, council-house tenants and those living in old industrial regions were the groups among which support for conservatism was weakest.[17] Such groups have been hit hardest by New Conservative policies: reductions in welfare benefits, the selling-off of public housing, and above all, mass unemployment. The stiffening of political opposition among these elements of the working class is scarcely surprising. It merely confirms the growing prevalence of a politics that is conducted without reference to a large alienated minority, which has insufficient power to make its presence count electorally.

Cross-class Support

These changing tendencies do not automatically denote the end of traditional 'class politics'. Class remains the single most important determinant of voting behaviour in Western Europe, and the New Conservatism itself represents the resuscitation of class politics in a new and virulent guise.[18] But it is also clear that the established parties increasingly have to appeal across conventional class lines in order to achieve governing majorities. Support for conservative prescriptions, whether of the neo-liberal or authoritarian variety, has been drawn from across the social spectrum.

Similarly, the electoral success of the *Front National* after 1986 was based on the combined support of diverse social elements. Polls conducted by the paper *Libération* at the 1986 French elections showed that 11 per cent of manual workers voted for Le Pen, a figure that appears to confirm journalistic impressions that the party recruited strongly among the unemployed, the unskilled and unorganised sections of the white working class, and – though this claim is more contentious – among disaffected Communist voters.[19]

But one should not overlook the significant array of 'respectable' middle-class groups ranged behind Le Pen: the self-employed urban petty bourgeoisie who provide the movement's rank-and-file, the military (the Le Pen vote among naval personnel at Toulon, for example, was embarrassingly conspicuous), and the well-to-do Catholics previously noted.[20] Le Pen's achievement, such as it was, was to mobilise the support of potentially reactionary elements in all social classes.

Region, Religion and Age

But class is not the only important variable in defining the social constituencies of the New Conservatism. Regional variations continue to be marked. Almost a decade of Thatcherism has hardened the political division in Britain between a largely Labour-dominated north and an overwhelmingly Conservative south. Similar, if less stark, are Belgium's traditional linguistic divisions – which have been compounded in the 1980s by the political division between a predominantly Liberal-Christian Democrat Flanders and a recalcitrantly Socialist Wallonia.

Religious differences likewise remain significant in shaping political behaviour – notably where Christian Democrat parties can still call upon reservoirs of Catholic support, as in Italy and West Germany. If the influence of some long-standing determinants of voting behaviour like religion does appear to be waning gradually, other social variables, like gender, may be taking their place. One of the more striking features of the 1987 British election, for example, was the decline in support for the Conservatives among women, in particular among women under 35.[21]

Finally, age itself has become a potent factor in the shifting patterns of voting behaviour. For with the exceptions of Britain and Scandinavia, the political outlook of West European youth appears to have veered steadily to the right. As with other variables the change has not been sudden, but it reflects in part the longer-term decline since the 1970s of the popularity of left parties among the young: the proportion of the 18–24 age group voting for the SPD in West Germany, for example, fell from 55 per cent to 39 per cent between 1972 and 1983.[22]

Since the mid-1980s, though, the trend towards conservatism in youth has become more pronounced and widespread. In 1987 Italy followed Germany with the emergence of the Christian Democrats as the most popular party among young voters, ending the long predominance of the Communist Party among this age group.[23] Portuguese youth similarly deserted the left in growing numbers after 1985, voting heavily for the neo-Thatcherite Cavaco Silva and the Social Democrats at the 1987 elections.[24] Nor have parties even further to the right lacked support among the young. Despite the strong anti-racist movement among French youth, it was estimated that one in seven students voted for Le Pen in the 1988 presidential elections.[25] Twenty years after 1968, large sections of West European youth have again shown themselves willing to lend support to radicalism: but this time they are supporting a radicalism of the right.

* * * *

To sum up, the forces of the New Conservatism do not rest on any single social constituency. As a form of mass politics it has cut across lines of class, religion and status to recruit support from all major social groups. This said, the New Conservatism has been notably successful in capturing key social groups. Where it has taken power it has managed to consolidate the middle-class vote, to weld together 'old' and 'new' middle classes into a cohesive electoral bloc. Within the working class, it has managed to establish a crucial base among the skilled workforce, to detach substantial sections of this group from their historical allegiance to parties of labour. It has likewise succeeded in attracting substantial support among youth, as a base for its future.

There is nothing inevitable or irreversible about these allegiances. There exists no natural constituency for the New Conservatism outside the ranks of big business and the wealthiest sections of the middle class. The support of an electoral majority (in some cases, not even *the* majority) must constantly be activated by the appeal to material interest and political 'common sense'. This process itself renders the whole project vulnerable. For the complex of popular attitudes and opinions which the New Conservatism seeks to bring together and articulate can be more ambiguous, and tenuous, than the picture of solid constituencies of support would suggest. To estimate the nature of support for the New Conservatism, and how far it has become a fixed feature on the European political map, we need to examine its appeal more closely.

The Appeal of the New Conservatism

Assessing why electoral groups have been attracted to the new forms of conservatism is more difficult than locating their social bases of support. Despite the battery of opinion polls and studies of voting behaviour available, it is hard to ascertain whether the shift to the right reflects a deep-lying 'value-change' among electorates, or if it is merely a temporary deviation from the social democratic path of post-war European politics. This in turn reflects the difficulty of linking social and political attitudes to voting decisions. Voting is rarely a matter of simple rational choice, even if material factors such as economic calculation invariably play a large part. Less tangible motives such as family tradition, religious affiliation, or the 'image' of the parties may influence the decisions of voters just as much as conventional political issues like economic policy.

This said, in assessing the appeal of the New Conservatism one cannot ignore signs of broad shifts in social attitudes. Not only is it clear that voting behaviour is shaped as much by everyday social experience as by events occurring in the narrow world of party politics. It has also been the frequent claim of the new varieties of conservatism that they are closer to the pulse of public opinion than traditional conservative or social democratic parties; that they articulate the 'real' concerns and aspirations of majority opinion in Western societies of the 1980s. Indeed, an essential part of the strategy of politicians like Chirac in France, Cavaco Silva in Portugal or Thatcher in Britain, has been to adapt their party's ideological appeal to perceived social changes in outlook and behaviour – while simultaneously seeking to direct or shape those changes in order to create a permanent majority for their brand of politics.

The nature of the conservative revolution in Western society is thus intimately bound up with the attempted marriage of political ideology with wider sets of social attitudes. In fact this marriage is not always an easy one, as we shall see. But to start with it is worth looking briefly at what might be termed the negative factors – the shifts in social attitudes that opened the way for a New Conservative politics.

Shifts in Political Opinion

Clearly, wherever New Conservative governments came to power in the late 1970s and early 1980s, their accession was predicated on substantial and significant shifts in public political opinion. In Britain prior to 1979, in West Germany to 1982 and in France to 1986, there was marked popular disaffection with key aspects of prevailing social democratic politics. This was most strongly registered over issues of state-influenced and interventionist economic policy.

Polls taken in France between 1980 and 1985 showed a sharp fall in the popular appeal of concepts specifically associated with social democratic economic management: 'planning', 'nationalisation', 'trade unions', 'socialism' – all of these reflected the 'wayward path' of the Mitterrand administration.[26] Polls taken in Britain prior to the 1979 election likewise showed a massive 75 per cent of respondents in favour of a reduction in state spending. Public esteem for trade unions, which were closely linked to the outgoing Labour administration's economic strategy through the ill-fated 'social contract', fell to its lowest recorded level since 1945.[27] Similarly, the fall of the West German SPD in Autumn 1982 coincided with a dramatic collapse of public confidence in the Schmidt administration's handling of the economy. A mere 9 per cent of SPD voters expressed optimism in the economic prospects for the following year; only 17 per cent of voters considered the SPD the party that guaranteed job security.[28]

What was sharply apparent from these various findings was a deep crisis of belief in the corporate model of economic management. It was expressed first as marked scepticism over continued state intervention in the economy – in itself, this was a major departure from an earlier consensus. Not only had post-1945 nationalisation programmes been universally popular, they had also formed part of a generally accepted framework of public ownership and state economic controls. Throughout Western Europe by 1960, Hobsbawm observed:

> The major question of policy was no longer whether or to what extent the State ought to enter the economy. It was how it should control the economy, how far it should refrain from taking over hitherto unoccupied "commanding heights" ...[29]

By the 1980s, this uniform consensus was no more than a minority faith. Only 21 per cent of those interviewed in a French poll of 1985 said that the Mitterrand government's nationalisations since 1981 could be considered a success. Almost 60 per cent declared them an outright failure, more bureaucratic and less efficient than private enterprise.[30] Likewise in social democratic Denmark and Norway, surveys revealed a steady build-up of opposition to public ownership and state intervention in the economy throughout the 1970s and early 1980s. Only in Sweden, it appears, has support for the economic aspects of collectivism remained firm.

Loss of Faith in Government

Further, a deep scepticism was expressed over the capacity of government to handle economic depression or mitigate its effects. This was most clearly evident in attitudes to mass unemployment. Surveys conducted in Britain in 1984 found that 55 per cent of respondents accepted that high unemployment was something 'we'll just have to learn to live with'. By 1984, only 4 per cent thought their children would find a job 'without any trouble', against some 46 per cent in 1965.[31] This strain of pessimism bordering on fatalism was widely registered: in West Germany, Finland, Austria and Norway as well as Britain, majorities were all recorded in 1984 who believed economic conditions would deteriorate rather than improve in 1985.[32]

But this scepticism was most acutely directed at the parties which laid greatest store by state management of the economy: social democratic and labour parties. Between February and November 1982 the proportion of the French electorate that thought Mitterrand's Socialist government was doing a 'rather' or 'very' bad job of handling France's economic problems rose from 41 per cent to 60 per cent.[33] A still more decisive rejection of social democratic management was evident in West Germany. Between 1980 and 1987 the SPD was was seen as less competent than the CDU on every question relating to the economy: unemployment, inflation, economic growth and even social security. Yet although this shift in opinion from left to right was clear enough, even the CDU lacked a majority of respondents who were sure of its competence on any economic matter.[34]

Voter Apathy

Lack of faith in government to solve the economic crisis reflected a more general loss of faith in the political system, as suggested by a widespread decline in support for the major parties. In many countries this has been a long-term trend, stretching back to the 1960s or earlier. But it has undoubtedly become more pronounced since the late 1970s.

In Italy, the proportion of voters abstaining in national elections rose from 6 to 11 per cent between 1976 and 1983. Significantly, abstention was most evident not in the south, where it has traditionally been highest, but in the northern industrial zones, the heartlands of the Socialist and Communist vote.[35] In Britain the proportion of the electorate voting remained more or less constant between 1970 and 1983, but the percentage voting for the traditional major parties, Labour and Conservative, declined from nearly 90 per cent to 70 per cent, partly as a result of the rise of the Liberals and SDP.[36] In 1983, for the first time in modern British electoral history, over half the voting population did not vote for one of the two main parties: either they voted for the new Liberal/SDP alliance, or else they stayed away.

Similarly, commentators on West Germany have noted sharp changes in political behaviour in the 1980s. For some what is distinctive is the emergence of new political values not represented by either of the two main party blocs, but instead by the Greens and neo-liberal FDP. This suggests a growing fragmentation of the party system. Other more perceptive observers have argued that what is most strikingly apparent is the diminishing credibility of the political process as a whole in the eyes of the electorate. Many Germans, according to Hans Magnus Enzensburger, now consider that society has become so complex and decentralised that politicians are of less and less relevance. Does it matter who is Chancellor, he suggests, 'if the commanding heights of government turn out to be only molehills'?[37]

A Culture of Anxiety

A waning belief in the political system in general and the traditional main parties in particular does not mean, however, that voters have become less concerned about political questions. On the contrary, the late 1970s and early 1980s was notable for signs of mounting public concern over law and order, the threat of war, race and 'permissiveness', as well as unemployment. A culture of anxiety emerged in which a perception of economic crisis easily spilled over into a sense of moral crisis.

In France, Britain and West Germany prior to the election of conservative governments, law and order came second only to unemployment in polls of the most pressing political issues among the voting public. Across EC countries generally, the rise in crime and terrorism proved to be the principal public fear in 1982, ahead of unemployment and environmental concerns. It was paralleled by mounting fears of war, caused by renewed tensions between the superpowers, and concern for national security among West European populations. These fears reached a peak in 1980 and did not subside until 1984.[38]

Racism also entered public discourse as a powerful symbol of social anxiety and 'moral decline'. A Gallup poll in January 1978 found that 61 per cent of respondents agreed with Thatcher's televised pronouncement that Britain was 'in danger of being swamped by people of different cultures'. Her personal popularity leapt 11 per cent in the immediate aftermath of the interview.[39] Similarly, polls taken in France after 1986 consistently showed between 20 and 30 per cent of the French electorate in broad agreement with the racist policies of Le Pen's *Front National*.[40] Such figures indicate that the rise to power of New Conservative governments has been preceded and accompanied by strong waves of anti-liberal sentiment. In the year prior to the election of the Chirac administration, polls showed that 89 per cent of the French population was indifferent or actively opposed to further measures of liberal social reform.[41]

* * * *

Loss of confidence in social democratic panaceas for the economy, a declining belief in the ability of parties or governments to manage the crisis or bring about political change, a pervasive sense of social and moral anxiety: all these elements played a part in preparing the ground for the rise to power of the New Conservatives in the 1970s and early 1980s. In so far as they reflected disillusionment over the corporate model of economic management, the extension of trade-union and bureaucratic state power, and 'permissive' social legislation, they worked against labour and social democratic parties. On the other hand, the existence of these 'negative' factors does not necessarily imply general or active acceptance of the kinds of policies identified with the New Conservatism. What then are the positive factors behind the New Conservatives' appeal?

Neo-liberalism

The most distinctive and far-reaching aspect of the New Conservatism has been its programme of economic neo-liberalism. On this score it appears to have attracted wide and plentiful support. The same French polls of 1980–5 that bore witness to the waning popularity of nationalisation and planning, also pointed to growing approval of terms associated with neo-liberal economics: 'capitalism', 'profit', 'free trade' and 'liberalism' itself. The term that evoked the most positive response of all (71 per cent) was 'competition', the universal key-word of neo-liberal panegyrics on the free market. The polls also showed a majority that considered that the 'liberal' path pursued by Thatcher and Reagan was more likely to lead to economic success than the social democratic model. Majority support for this view was found among all social groups, most markedly among business and the liberal professions, but also among workers.[42] Similarly, a comfortable majority was in favour of the Thatcherite proposition that 'government can't do much to create prosperity; it is up to people to help themselves' in a British survey in 1983.[43]

Unfortunately, few comparable surveys of the ideological reception of economic neo-liberalism exist. This in itself is partly explained by the manifest success of parties stressing the values of the free market: competition, enterprise, individualism. As I have already described, as a matter of policy the idea of economic liberalisation has become all but hegemonic in Western Europe in the 1980s; so opposition is phrased in terms of degree rather than outright contradiction or countermand.

But on specific questions such as tax cuts and privatisation, the New Conservatism has found clear constituencies of support across conventional party divides. Tax cuts have not surprisingly had an almost universal appeal, even if by the mid-1980s it was apparent in states like Denmark, Norway and Britain that voters were increasingly reluctant to see them traded for cuts in public services.

Privatisation also appears to have met increasing approval where it has been most strongly projected. In Britain the shift in favour was particularly dramatic: in October 1974, support for further nationalisation outstripped that for privatisation by 32 to 22 per cent; by 1983, however, the situation had been comprehensively reversed, with 42 per cent in favour of privatisation and only 18 per cent for further nationalisation.[44] A similar majority was found in France in 1985, with 43 per cent in support of privatisation of nationalised industries and 33 per cent against.[45]

Measures associated with economic liberalisation therefore appear to have wide and substantial constituencies in Western Europe. Moreover, the case of France and Britain suggests that this support transcends traditional divides of class and party, a point which has not been lost on politicians of either left or right. New Conservative ministers like Edouard Balladur and Lord Young claim this is proof of the appeal of 'popular capitalism'. Alternatively, spokesmen of the social democratic left like Peter Glotz of the SPD say it affirms the Europe-wide 'trend to individualisation', identified with the combined effects on the working class of educational mobility, rising incomes and the decentralisation of the work-place.[46] Neither of these conclusions need to be taken as entirely definitive. What such polls most strongly indicate is primarily the growth in opposition to the State and its intervention in the economy, whether in the private sphere (taxation) or the public (nationalisation). Outside the domain of public services, private enterprise has come invariably to be seen as more efficient and more responsive to the demands of both the consumer and of technological change. In this limited though significant sense, the call of 'rolling back the State' reflects and condenses wider shifts in political attitudes.

A Hard Image

There are also signs that the 'hard' image of the New Conservatism, and of its leaders in particular, has found a receptive audience at a time of economic recession and heightened public sensitivity to issues of law and order. This partially explains the preference of Italian business for the 'modernising' Craxi over the 'traditionalist' De Mita. It has also enabled leaders such as Thatcher and Cavaco Silva to discount complaints of authoritarianism, and present their anti-labour and privatisation measures as radical, democratic and progressive. Such an image allowed Cavaco Silva to push through measures reducing job security, breaking up collective farms and initiating the privatisation of state-owned companies and newspapers in 1987, while maintaining a positive rating of 69 per cent in November opinion polls.[47] In Britain, a Gallup poll found majority support in 1983 in favour of the proposition that politicians should 'stick firmly to their beliefs' in the face of opposition, rather than compromise.[48] So the rejection of a consensual approach seems to be broadly accepted as an inevitable and necessary component of New Conservative political leadership – a contributory factor in its appeal.

The image of strong leadership has likewise strengthened conservative claims to be the party of law and order. In countries where terrorism has been a live political issue in the 1970s and 1980s – Italy, West Germany, France, Spain, Belgium, Britain to name only the more obvious – parties of the right have benefited from public anxieties. In a 1978 poll West Germans named 'terrorism' as the third 'greatest problem in Europe', after unemployment and 'economic problems'.[49] Similarly in Britain, 91 per cent of respondents considered terrorism a 'serious world problem' in 1985; compared with 85 per cent in 1979. On both occasions over 70 per cent considered governments had been too 'soft' on terrorists, a figure which tallies more widely with public sentiment in Europe.[50]

A 'hard line' on terrorism, and law and order more generally, thus draws on a large reservoir of support around an issue that comes second only to the economy as a source of electoral concern in most European states. The FDP/CDU/CSU coalition that has governed West Germany since 1982 has undoubtedly gained electoral sustenance from the way the population identifies the CSU and its leader, the ebullient Franz-Josef Strauss, with opposition to communism, terrorism and immigration; in the process the CSU has undercut a potential resurgence of support for the far-right NPD. Equally, the British Conservatives have benefited since the Thatcher takeover in 1975 from a consistent lead over Labour in opinion polls on all questions of law and order and national defence.

Limitations of Conservative Appeal

Nevertheless, the 'hard' image of the New Conservatism carries its own political risks. Leaders such as Thatcher, Cavaco Silva and Wilfrid Maartens have all been censured for their authoritarian style. Thatcher's ratings as a strong, decisive leader increased steadily between 1977 and 1985, but the perception of her political divisiveness rose even more markedly over the same period.[51] Maartens's dictatorial style was a significant factor in his government's defeat in the 1987 Belgian elections.

Moreover, the 'hard' image may backfire when conservative leaders fail to deliver. The credibility of Chirac's presidential bid in 1988 was weakened by his government's humiliating climbdown over educational and trade-union reform, which was amplified by the persistent presence of an indubitable 'hard man' – Le Pen – to the right. All this suggests that in so far as electorates are prepared to tolerate the authoritarian style of leadership commonly identified with the New Conservatism, this must be both effective, and relatively discreet. The ascendancy of Thatcher has rarely looked more vulnerable than when her dictatorial style has been exposed to public view, as happened briefly during the Westland affair of 1986.[52]

But there are other more substantial limitations to the appeal of the New Conservatism than those based merely on image. For if the New Conservatism has managed to reflect and condense shifting attitudes on a number of crucial political issues, the evidence indicates that on others, public opinion is strongly resistant to conservative prescriptions.

The most important of these lies in popular support for the welfare state, and opposition to measures that appear to threaten it. A poll in May 1985 in France showed a strong majority (69 per cent) opposed to the suggestion that the existing social security system should be replaced by a scheme of voluntary insurance. A similar majority (66 per cent) was likewise against the idea that the state-enforced minimum wage should be suppressed in order to stimulate youth employment.[53] Since the mid-1980s public enthusiasm for tax cuts has waned in states like Norway, Denmark, the Netherlands and Belgium, when these were set against cuts in public services. In Britain, the proportion of respondents prepared to countenance an increase in taxation to extend welfare and education services rose sharply from 34 per cent to 59 per cent between 1979 and 1985. By 1985, 89 per cent thought the government should put more money into the National Health Service, while only 20 per cent thought it should encourage private medicine.[54] Given this volume of public feeling it is not surprising that New Conservative plans to reform the welfare state have had to be shelved in one country after another across Western Europe.

Second, there appears to be more public enthusiasm for economic liberalism in theory than in practice. Thus, while the liberal 'model' was widely seen in France as a magic cure for economic ills in the mid-1980s, support for measures to facilitate the dismissal of workers or to remove price controls was very much more muted.[55] The actual experience of New Conservative government after 1986 did little to dissolve these reservations, judging by the results of the 1988 presidential and national elections.

But in many cases the vein of public scepticism over New Conservative economic recipes for success appears to run still deeper. Just as in the United States the mounting trade deficit casts a shadow of doubt over the efficacy of Reaganite panaceas, so in Britain a significant proportion of the population seems to remain distrustful of the Thatcher government's claims to be presiding over an economic renaissance. In 1985, six years into the 'economic miracle', 42 per cent of those asked thought the economy would continue to deteriorate under Conservative policies; as against only 23 per cent who felt it would improve.[56] Even in the foremost states of the conservative revolution, in other words, substantial sections of the population have remained unconvinced of its economic prescriptions.

Lastly, there is little evidence that the social values identified with the New Conservatism, such as thrift or the work ethic, have taken root in wider populations. Many of the advanced capitalist countries, in which the real incomes of wealthier social groups have continued to rise, have seen an unprecedented boom in credit and consumer spending during the 1980s and a consequent squeeze on personal savings. Both Britain and the USA have been conspicuous in this regard. Consumerism, associated through advertising with the image of the enterprise culture, has proved to be a far more potent source of appeal for the New Conservatism than the incentive to save, at least when the rate of inflation remains low.

Nor is there any apparent widespread desire for a restoration of the nineteenth-century work ethic. Polls in France in the mid-1980s showed strong support for a further reduction of the working week to 35 hours. Only the business community did not concur.[57] Indeed, in West Germany and the Netherlands, right-wing governments have been forced by trade unions to reduce statutory working hours, in order to compensate for declining real wages among workers.

Furthermore, despite the widely registered sentiment, capitalised upon by conservatives, in favour of a return to 'traditional values', there is little sign that this translates into a 'moral majority' when it comes to specific issues. In Catholic Italy in 1981 an attempt to reverse by a referendum the 1978 law legalising abortion failed. The scale of support for the pro-abortion lobby (68 per cent) was a humiliating defeat for the Christian Democrats, who were largely associated with this attempt at moral revisionism.[58] The level of popular scepticism about the moral authority of government is, though, perhaps best summed up by a British poll asking respondents what they thought politicians meant by the phrase 'a return to traditional values'. The majority (53 per cent) replied 'nothing', or more cynically, 'means what they want it to mean'.[59]

The Balance Sheet

Clearly, then, despite wide current appeal, there is no sense in which the New Conservatism could be said to have rooted itself in popular attitudes in Western Europe; even in societies like Britain where it has enjoyed unbroken political dominance for almost a decade. It is vulnerable in its authoritarianism, in its claims to the moral high-ground, and in its commitment to 'roll back the State' in the specific domains of education, health and welfare. More broadly, this brief comparative survey of social attitudes suggests that in accounting for the appeal of the New Conservatism the 'negative' factors have been more significant than the 'positive'. In other words, the shift to the right in Western Europe during the 1980s is less a direct reflection of the appeal of the economic and social prescriptions of the New Conservatism, than of a widespread disenchantment with key aspects of the post-war social democratic consensus – and most obviously, with pre-existing forms of state intervention in the economy.

None the less, the impact of New Conservative ideology on policy-makers and electorates across Western Europe over the last decade has been profound. In one state after another, more or less conspicuously, it has succeeded in redefining the basic ideological assumptions on which politics is conducted and policy made. As the next chapter will make clear, there no longer exists at governmental level in Western Europe a clear alternative to the model of free-market capitalism combined with increasing state power. This new institutional consensus has been reached against the background of a prolonged international economic crisis, which also brought about a crisis of political and social legitimation. The crisis of legitimation has been expressed simultaneously through a decline of belief in the political system, and through rising anxiety on social and moral issues.

The New Conservative answer to this conjuncture is clear cut: the promotion of free-market capitalism and the contraction of the State's role, to hasten economic restructuring on the one hand; and the simultaneous expansion of state power, to shore up social and political authority on the other. It is a response that appears to correspond both with the demands of the crisis itself and public perceptions of it. In its own terms it is both logical and electorally viable.

At the same time, it is only one of a range of potential political responses to the conjuncture. The ambivalence of public opinion regarding many conservative policy prescriptions is evidence of a broad popular sense that there are other ways of thinking about the crisis, and other paths to its resolution, however vaguely these may be formulated. New Conservative parties have not as yet entirely persuaded electorates that theirs is the only answer to the crisis.

However, the fact that no new alternative answer has as yet been taken on by electorates to anything like the same degree, points to the New Conservatives' ability to condense complex political questions and equally complex public responses into a cohesive working ideology. Out of it a new political 'common sense' can be formulated, capable in its coherence and simplicity of overriding the vagaries and ambiguities of 'public opinion'. Support is then dependent not on an active embracing of New Conservative philosophy – its swallowing whole by a gullible public – but on its more limited acceptance as the only practicable 'common sense' available.

The predominance of this 'common sense' is then sustained by a number of factors. First, in electoral terms ideological hegemony is irrelevant, since it is only necessary to gain the consent of a majority of voters. Indeed, in many of Western Europe's multi-party systems a minority will suffice. Second, the New Conservatism has succeeded in obtaining cross-class support, both electorally and for specific programmes like economic liberalisation. This enables it plausibly to claim mass support and to be representing the 'national interest'. Third, it has capitalised on the cross-class disillusionment with policies identified with traditional social democracy, and on the subsequent turmoil on the left about how best to confront the right's revolution.

It was in the ideological space created by this widespread disillusionment, and in the left's incapacity to renew the social democratic enterprise, that both the libertarian and authoritarian seeds of the New Conservatism were planted. In short, the West European left has been deeply implicated in the shift to the right during the 1970s and 1980s.

4

Playing the Game – The Role of the Left in Europe

Advance or Retreat?

For over a decade the future of the left in Western Europe has been the subject of anxious debate. Prophecies of the impending 'death of socialism' have emanated not only from the triumphant right; similar voices have also been heard on the left. By the late 1970s intellectuals in France, Italy, West Germany and Britain were composing a series of historical epilogues: the end of ideology, of class, of the labour movement. What Gorz, Touraine, Althusser, Hobsbawm and others all sought to convey was the passing of the socialist moment, at least in the forms of mass movement and class struggle with which it had become classically identified in Europe.[1]

A more literal, though none the less historical, overview suggests otherwise. The period since the 1960s, it has been argued, has brought marked advances for the working class and for radicalism on several fronts.[2] Rates of unionisation reached new peaks in many European countries during the 1970s, and were combined with a growth in power at the point of production and an increased preparedness to use industrial muscle for material and political ends, notably in Britain, Belgium, Italy and Spain. Socialist parties also registered substantial gains, achieving peak levels of support in West Germany and Austria in the 1970s, and in France, Greece, Italy, Portugal and Spain in the 1980s. The gains carried socialist parties to office in all these countries, in several cases for the first time since the 1930s.

In addition, this period witnessed the burgeoning of new social forces. These grew out of the student revolt of the late 1960s, but they emerged widely and powerfully in the 1980s in the peace, ecology and women's movements. From this viewpoint, the defeats inflicted on the trade unions and socialist parties by the right in the 1980s would appear localised and likely to be short-lived.

But neither of these contradictory interpretations is particularly convincing. The projected demise of the labour movement and industrial struggle seems premature, to say the least, in the light of the wave of strikes against the Kohl government's trade-union legislation in 1985–6, or the British miners' strike of 1984–5, the longest major industrial conflict in modern European history. The predicted 'end of class' likewise appears singularly inappropriate at a moment when right-wing governments have consciously set out to undermine the traditional institutions of working-class power, and are by their policies hastening the expansion and recreation of a new 'underclass'.

However, it would be equally misleading to present the 1970s and 1980s as decades of indubitable advance for the working class, or political radicalism. In the first place, political parties of the left have been – and continue to be – deeply implicated in the shift to the right in European politics. Simply to enumerate the accession to power of socialist parties overlooks the qualitative performance of those parties in government, and their part in preparing the ground for, or even practising, the forms of politics earlier defined as New Conservative. It is no longer self-evident, in other words, that the programmes of socialist parties – in or out of government – are socialist in any recognisable sense.

Further, the optimistic view of the state of the left today ignores the changing relations between elements on the left: between parties and trade unions, and between these and the new social movements. The effectiveness of the left as a whole obviously depends on the relative coherence of these essential components. Their current fragmentation is another reason to doubt the proposition of a socialist advance.

While it is not necessary to accept the wilder diagnoses that socialism is in a terminal condition, it is hard to dispute that structurally, electorally and ideologically, socialism is in crisis. That crisis is in large measure both the cause and effect of the resurgence of the right. Moreover, it is possible to speak broadly of a crisis of the left across Western Europe, rather than a series of politically or nationally distinct 'crises'. As an historian of Italian politics observed in 1987, 'the symmetry between the vicissitudes of the various components of the European left is profound.'[3] How this predicament developed, how it paved the way for the revitalised conservatism that then transformed the political map, and how the European left has subsequently responded to the challenge is the subject of this chapter.

The Traditional Parties of Labour

Parties in Crisis

During the 1970s and early 1980s, a number of the major traditional parties of labour, the British Labour Party, The West German Social Democrats (SPD) and the Italian Communist Party (PCI), all entered acute political difficulties. Except in the PCI, the dimensions of the problem were not fully apparent at the time, even to those in the parties themselves. Each of the three parties had held power in the 1970s – the PCI, through its unofficial coalition with the Christian Democrats embodied in the 'historic compromise'. By 1982, each had been replaced in office by parties to their right. None has regained power, or even looked like approaching it, since.

These developments were significant for a number of reasons. First, all three parties had lengthy historical traditions, and had acquired an important symbolic status within the international labour movement. The British Labour Party was recognised for its singular amalgamation of labour's industrial and political interests, and alongside the Swedish Social Democratic Labour Party, for its pioneering role in the formation of post-war welfare socialism. The German SPD had immense leverage as Europe's oldest socialist party; indeed, it has been widely acknowledged as 'the most important political party in Europe'.[4] The PCI has been Western Europe's most powerful and creative Communist party in the post-war period. It was the major architect of the distinctive brand of 'Eurocommunism' whose influence was widely registered, particularly on the Mediterranean left, during the 1970s. The adversities these parties have subsequently suffered have, consequently, had repercussions beyond the confines of their specific national political cultures.

But what is also significant is the similarity of the circumstances in which each party's crisis occurred. Both the German SPD and Britain's Labour had held office for most of the period between the mid-1960s and 1980, and were therefore accepted parties of government. As the major party of opposition in Italy, the PCI had steadily increased its share of the vote since the 1950s, and appeared capable by the mid-1970s of breaking the post-war dominance of the Christian Democrats.

By 1980, however, each party was riven by internal division. Still more damaging, all had succeeded in alienating large sections of their natural constituency – the working class, the labour movement, youth – by their handling of the economic and social predicament. In so doing, they left the way open for their replacement by parties to the right, which subsequently implemented radically regressive political programmes. The character of these separate crises and their common features will become more evident if we examine each case in greater detail.

The British Labour Party

It was in the British Labour Party that the malaise was first apparent, and where it has continued to be most critical. Unlike most parties of the European left, Labour's historical tradition was largely uninfluenced by Marxism. The party was formed, tardily and reluctantly, at the behest of the skilled craft unions. It was essentially a response to the spate of anti-union legislation at the turn of the twentieth century.

From the outset, the party's role was conceived as limited and defensive: to preserve the legal rights of organised labour by establishing a permanent working-class presence in Parliament. Within the party, industrial and political activity were strictly demarcated: the party kept a conspicuously low profile, for example, in the unprecedented explosion of industrial militancy prior to the First World War and during the short-lived General Strike of 1926. In short, from its inception the party was envisaged as a means to preserve existing interests rather than as a vehicle of social transformation.[5]

Apart from this inherent 'labourism', the party's ideology was informed by a mixture of radical liberalism and fabianism. Its main contribution to the post-1945 order, the welfare state and the mixed economy, was the work not of socialist policy-makers but of staunch members of the liberal establishment, Beveridge and Keynes. The party's fabian bent, characterised by a bureaucratic emphasis on 'reform from above', was evident in the way it carried out the post-war programme of nationalisation. The newly nationalised industries were set up on the model of public corporations, earlier devised for the BBC. In most cases the former owners were simply co-opted onto the new boards of management. No provisions were made for the representation of workers in the industries concerned, and Labour ministers came out firmly against the merest suggestion of workers' control.

The post-war Labour administration, therefore, did not seek any significant transformation of the relationship between labour and capital. Nor did it recognise the fundamental weakness of British capitalism until the 1960s, when the Wilson government made a belated attempt at modernisation. This was conceived in true fabian tradition as 'modernisation from above'. It involved institutional reform of the civil service and education, a programme of liberal social legislation, and central planning on the French model, directed by 'experts'. Again, no further change in the existing relations between labour and capital was envisaged because, as Wilson unhesitatingly asserted, 'capitalism could provide affluence for the working class while at the same time preserving the gains of the well-to-do.'[6]

Unfortunately, Wilson's logic did not not coincide with that of capital itself. When the projected economic modernisation faltered in the face of sluggish growth-rates, the flight of capital and devaluation in the later 1960s, the Labour government turned on the trade unions, by seeking to enforce legally binding wage limits and threatening to outlaw unofficial strikes. The contradiction between the party's role as the political representative of organised labour and its preparedness to sacrifice those commitments in the interest of British capital was finally exposed, contributing to its electoral defeat in 1970.

Wilson's grandiose blueprint for the modernisation of British economy and society was never revived on the left. When Labour returned to office in 1974, it was as the only available government capable of controlling the trade unions, which were then at the peak of their power after their defeat of the Heath administration. So the Labour leaders saw their task as a holding operation. The outline of an 'alternative economic strategy', promoted by the party's left and promising 'a fundamental and irreversible shift in the balance of power and wealth in favour of working people and their families',[7] was quietly shelved by the leadership, on the convenient grounds that the government lacked the working majority in Parliament to pass radical policies. Instead, Labour projected as the centrepiece of its programme the more modest idea of the 'social contract', in which increases in state welfare would be exchanged for wage restraint on the part of the trade unions.

From there on the government followed the same path as its predecessors, its energies swallowed up in the conduct of crisis management. As the international capitalist recession continued to squeeze an already weak British economy, so old remedies were compounded with new, more desperate measures. Deflation was succeeded by the negotiation of an International Monetary Fund (IMF) loan, which in turn entailed cuts in public expenditure, including welfare, and a rapid rise in unemployment to 1.5 million. The whole political debacle culminated in the 'winter of discontent' of 1978–9, when the unions, exasperated by public-sector cuts and declining real wages, abandoned the 'social contract', and began a succession of mass pay strikes. Unable to deliver even on its elementary promise to palliate the unions, Labour's credibility as the 'natural party of government' collapsed.

The trajectory of the Labour Party from the 1960s is instructive on several counts. First, many of its policies directly anticipated those which later came to be seen as central components of the New Conservatism. After 1976 'monetarism', in the form of strict control of the money supply combined with reductions in public-sector spending, became the guiding principle of Labour's fiscal policy, under the tutelage of Chancellor Healey at the IMF's behest. The same years also saw the introduction of the first significant cuts in welfare. And as a number of critics have correctly pointed out, it was the Labour government of Wilson in the late 1960s, not the radical right of the 1970s, that first singled out the trade unions as the principal obstacle to Britain's economic rejuvenation.[8]

But the political space that opened for Thatcherism in the 1980s was as much a product of what Labour had failed to do over the previous two decades, as of what it actually did in office. Labour's failure lay not simply in its inability to institute effective economic modernisation. No government since the war, including that of Thatcher, was able to halt its precipitous decline up to 1987. What is clear, however, is that once the brief spark of hope, illuminated by Wilson's promise of a new society, forged in the 'white heat of technological revolution' had been extinguished, the Labour leadership reneged on any planned, structural renovation of Britain. It was not merely that it rejected the alternative economic strategy of its left wing out of hand, but that it could offer in its place no alternative conception of how the economic crisis could be met or overcome.

This lack of imaginative political will or vision was equally evident in social policy. After the considerable programme of reform encompassing liberal legislation on divorce, abortion and homosexuality, and the expansion of educational opportunity under the first Wilson administration, no further sustained attack on social inequality was envisaged. The implementation of the Equal Pay Act and measures against sexual and racial discrimination after 1975 were significant advances, but they were conceived at an earlier period or as piecemeal concessions, not as part of any concerted transformation of Britain's archaic class structure. Nor even was there any attempt, as in Sweden, to update or extend the welfare state, Labour's perceived historic contribution. By the 1970s Britain's welfare benefits were among the lowest in Western society.

Labour's uninspiring record in office had repercussions on both the party and its wider social constituency. During the 1970s, divisions began to open up between left and right within the party. The left rallied behind the alternative economic strategy, and strove to make the parliamentary leadership more accountable to the party as a whole. After Labour's election defeat in 1979 the constitutional conflict resulted in formal victory for the left, but also led to defections on the right and the setting up of a new centre party, the Social Democratic Party (SDP). Nor was this the end of the matter, for while divisions between left and right have continued to plague the party through the 1980s, the existence of a third force occupying the 'middle ground' of British politics persists in damaging Labour's electoral prospects.

Still more serious were signs in the 1970s that Labour was not only losing its hold over its traditional constituencies, it was also failing to attract new ones. The austerity measures implemented after 1976 hit the working class hardest, and suggested that – as in the late 1960s – when forced, the party leadership would always choose to protect the interests of capital over those of labour. The alienation of Labour's working-class constituencies was powerfully indicated by the strikes of predominantly unskilled workers during the 'winter of discontent', and the massive swing to the Conservatives among skilled workers at the 1979 election.

At the same time the party failed to extend its bases of support among the expanding white-collar and service sector, or among groups actively carving out distinct social identities: women, blacks, youth. Throughout the 1970s Labour's campaigns remained resolutely – though less and less successfully – directed at the white, male, skilled, worker. Labour continued largely oblivious of any social identities or interests forged outside the traditional industrial heartlands and their corresponding labour organisations.

The demise of the Labour Party since the 1970s offers the most spectacular example of the crisis affecting parties of the left in contemporary Western Europe. But critics would be mistaken in imagining that it has been exceptional. What is striking about Labour's experience is not its uniqueness, but how much it corresponds to the problems afflicting socialist parties elsewhere. Even in the later 1970s and early 1980s, long-established parties like the West German SPD and the Italian PCI were encountering similar difficulties with similar results. Almost all the problems besetting Labour over the last two decades – internal party divisions, a deteriorating relationship with organised labour and the working class, the perception of the party as bureaucratic, unresponsive and outmoded – can be found to a greater or lesser degree on the continental left. It is equally impossible to overlook the way in which these weaknesses contributed to the revitalisation of conservatism.

The West German SPD

Historically, the West German SPD has a very different lineage from that of the Labour Party. Yet since the 1960s the political and ideological fortunes of the two parties have followed an increasingly parallel course. The key development permitting this convergence was the Bad Godesberg Conference of 1959, at which the SPD formally renounced its Marxist inheritance and affirmed its transition to a Western-style social democratic party, by publicly endorsing the existing political and economic order. Specifically, this meant not only accepting the social market economy laid down by Erhard immediately after the war, and withdrawing proposals for extended public ownership, but also sanctioning the key coordinates of post-1945 foreign policy, including membership of the EC and NATO.

The process that transformed the SPD from a class party to a *Volkspartei* after 1959, and from there to the 'natural party of government' bears more than a passing resemblance to Wilson's attempt to recast Labour as the party of technocratic modernisation in the early 1960s. Within the SPD the passage from a party of radical reform to a party of accommodation was given characteristic theoretical underpinning by Brandt in 1961:

> In a sound and developing democracy, it is the norm rather than the exception that the parties put forward similar, even identical, demands in a number of fields. The question of priorities in the rank order of tasks to be solved ... thus becomes ever so much more the content of opinion formation.[9]

Leaving aside the more cynical connotations of 'opinion formation', it is clear that the ambition of the SPD leadership was now confined to competing with the conservative parties, not over substantive differences of policy or principle, but over who could provide the most effective management of the capitalist economy: the most efficient 'rule by experts'.

This trend was consolidated in 1966, when the SPD came to power for the first time since Weimar, in the 'Grand Coalition' with the CDU/CSU. The party was confirmed as a reliable and pragmatic partner in government, and it began to evolve its own technocratic style of corporate management, bringing employers and union representatives into the process of economic policy-making.

But just as in Britain Labour began to encounter resistance from its own traditional bases of support in the late 1960s, so too did the SPD. A large section of the German labour movement (including the SPD's closest union allies, the *Deutscher Gewerkschaftsbund* – DGB) had opposed the party's entry into the Grand Coalition from the outset, aware that any residual capacity for reform would be minimised. This was indeed the case: the party's more progressive social policies were shelved. Worse was to follow in 1968, when the SPD agreed to the Emergency Laws that gave the State extended powers to act 'in the event of a threat to national security and public order'. Support for the Emergency Laws enabled the SPD to pose as the guardian of law and order, but this met with massive opposition from the trade unions and the swelling student movement.

The immediate political crisis was solved by the formation of the new Social Liberal coalition in 1969. The SPD was now a senior partner in alliance with the Free Democratic Party (FDP), with Brandt as Chancellor. The right wing of the party was satisfied by the vindication of its long-term strategy for power; the left by Brandt's stated commitment to a programme of reform. But the honeymoon was brief, as the logic of the politics of accommodation gradually reasserted its grip, and was reinforced by the onset of international economic recession.

The implementation of Brandt's *Ostpolitik* in the early 1970s, aimed at re-establishing relations with the German Democratic Republic and the Eastern bloc, marked a welcome break with the rigid anti-Communism of post-war foreign policy. But it was carried out at the expense of, rather than alongside, the promised programme of domestic reform. Educational and tax reform as well as the abortion-law liberalisation that the left demanded were all postponed, on grounds of cost and potential conflict with the FDP. Moreover, the spirit of the Emergency Laws was revived in even more pernicious form when the government introduced the *Berufsverbot*, the strict political vetting of applicants for state employment, starting with the 'decree on radicals' in January 1972.[10]

After 1974, however, the shift of the SPD leadership towards repressive pragmatism became inexorable. It was symbolised by the emergence of Helmut Schmidt as Chancellor, the new technocracy personified, who prided himself on his adherence to tight-fisted realism, which he justified by sanctimonious references to 'the sober passion of practical reason'.[11] Under Schmidt, all thought of progressive policy-making was subordinated to considerations of narrow economic expediency – 'crisis management' of a notably conservative variety. Monetary stringency and limits on public expenditure became the order of the day. Promises to extend industrial democracy, vocational training and pension schemes were suspended.

As Schmidt increasingly surrounded himself with bankers and industrialists, so predictably the government's economic policies gave priority to the demands of capital over the needs of labour.[12] Meanwhile, with the growth of political terrorism, the apparatus of civil repression was maintained and extended. To all intents and purposes, the policies of the Schmidt administration had become indistinguishable in practice from those of the conservative CDU/CSU.

Opposition from the left to the government's strategy was slower to show itself in West Germany than in Britain. For most of the 1970s, criticism within the SPD was held in check by Brandt, party chairman after 1974. Brandt acted as mediator between the leadership and the left. But by 1980, severe criticism of the Schmidt regime began to be voiced on a number of issues. The government's proposal to proceed with the deployment of Cruise and Pershing missiles met fierce resistance – both from within the SPD and from the rapidly growing peace movement. The party leadership was forced to postpone a decision on the missiles until 1983. A similar compromise had earlier been reached in 1977, restricting the government's plans for the expansion of nuclear energy. Yet the question refused to go away, and Schmidt was forced to defend the nuclear programme by playing it off against the issue of unemployment.

Most damaging, however, was the opposition that emerged over economic policy itself. The conflict came to a head in 1981 when, under pressure from the FDP, and in a rapidly deteriorating economic climate, the government introduced an 'austerity programme' that cut social benefits while making tax concessions to business. With unemployment at 1.25 million and rising, the move provoked a storm of criticism from the trade unions, notably the powerful metalworkers' union *IG Metall*, which threatened to withdraw further support for the government. The left of the SPD reacted similarly, arguing that the government had finally abandoned altogether the fundamental principles of economic justice that had been enunciated at Bad Godesburg.

But what the crisis no less exposed was the lack of any clear strategy behind economic policy other than short-term expedience. Although it had based its bid for office on the narrow claim of being the most efficient manager of the capitalist economy, the SPD leadership had no broader vision of a socialist project with which to appeal to the party or the electorate once that claim to efficiency was in doubt. In the event, accusations of a 'theory deficit' consistently levelled at the the Schmidt leadership by the party's left proved justified.[13] The emperor indeed had no clothes.

From this account, comparisons with Britain are self-evident. It was not simply FDP's conversion to thoroughgoing economic liberalism and its defection from the Social Liberal coalition that spelled the end for the Schmidt government. Through its embrace of international economic orthodoxy, combining 'monetarist' controls with fiscal restraint, and its ready identification with the apparatus of civil repression at home and NATO abroad, the Schmidt administration itself paved the way for the accession of Kohl and the CDU/CSU in 1982.

The logic for the SPD's course was provided not only by the international capitalist recession after 1974, but equally by the party's own political trajectory since Bad Godesburg. In adopting an ever more technocratic style of government, the SPD leadership became less and less identifiable with any distinctive political project. The pressures of economic recession only hastened the process by which the party's policies in office came to seem interchangeable with those of the centre-right. In this position, the SPD under Schmidt fell foul of the system's inherent logic: once the political process is reduced to a matter of who can manage the capitalist economy more efficiently, those parties that represent capital most closely are always likely to win out at times of recession.

The decline of the SPD from the mid-1970s has had significant repercussions on the German left. Unlike the British Labour Party in the same period, the SPD did not suffer from sustained in-fighting. After Schmidt's resignation in 1982, the party rallied round, though the subsequent attempt to give it a fresh identity and political direction has been a protracted process.

More immediately damaging was the leadership's handling of the nuclear energy and NATO missiles issues, which opened a split between the party and the ecology and peace movements, and hastened the emergence of the Green Party as an independent political force after 1980. Not only did the SPD fail to incorporate the new social movements into its programme, but experience of the later Schmidt administration had also alienated traditional

support in the organised working class. The massive defections of
blue-collar workers to the CDU/CSU in old heavy-industry areas
such as the Rhine and the Rühr was one of the features of the
1983 election. All in all, the experience of the late 1970s and early
1980s can scarcely be said to have been less disastrous for the SPD
than for the British Labour Party, even if the circumstances of its
defeat were less strife-torn and dramatic.

The Italian PCI

Lastly, the late 1970s was a period of crisis for a third major force on
the West European left, the PCI. As a Communist party nominally
linked to Moscow until 1981, and with an unbroken commitment
to Marxism, the formation of the PCI would appear very different
from the British Labour Party and the West German SPD. But in fact
there are significant parallels between the PCI's political
development and that of these other parties since 1960. The
problems facing the PCI in the 1980s have been commensurate
with the difficulties experienced by many socialist parties in
Western Europe.

Like Labour and the SPD, the PCI emerged from the Second
World War as a mass party, with strong roots in the industrial
working class. Even before its expulsion from government in 1947
at the onset of the Cold War, the party leadership under Togliatti
was insisting on the right to pursue an 'Italian road to socialism',
replacing Lenin with Gramsci as its principal theoretician, and
substituting the concept of 'progressive democracy' for that of
revolutionary struggle.

Like the SPD, the PCI continued to oppose membership of NATO
and the EC in the 1950s, while endorsing the system of
parliamentary democracy. Unlike the SPD, the PCI made no formal
dissociation from the party's Marxist inheritance, nor did it publicly
embrace moderate social democracy, as the SPD had done at Bad
Godesburg. Rather, the PCI's path towards an idiosyncratic form of
radical reformism was signalled by a series of shifting strategies: from
Togliatti's 'progressive democracy' and 'polycentrism' in the 1950s,
to Berlinguer's elaboration of the 'historic compromise' and
'Eurocommunism' in the 1970s.[14]

The particular trajectory of the PCI in the 1950s and 1960s was
shaped, not only by the internal strategy of the party, but also by
the political environment in which it developed. In the immediate
post-war decades both the SPD in Germany and the PCI in Italy
were forced to operate in political systems dominated by Christian
Democracy – the 'CD State'. With the exception of the PCI's brief

participation in post-war coalition government, both parties remained out of power for two decades after 1945, while they steadily gathered electoral strength.

For the SPD leadership, Bad Godesberg was less a response to a sense of permanent marginality than a recognition that power was within reach – a prospect that became reality with the party's entry into the Grand Coalition in 1966. For the PCI, on the other hand, the slower build-up of electoral strength meant that the prospect of power did not emerge for a further decade. So the PCI was able to continue defining its political direction in terms of broad strategy, rather than precise policies. Until the early 1970s the attainment of political office remained remote.

At the same time, there were clear signs that the PCI was following the pattern of other West European left parties, in accommodating itself to the existing political order. During the early 1960s it dropped its former opposition to EC-membership for Italy, and by the mid-1970s it had likewise reversed its position on NATO. Indeed, during the student protests of 1968 and the 'hot autumn' of industrial militancy of 1969, the PCI faced a barrage of criticism from both workers and students, of its increasingly moderate and bureaucratic character.[15] In the 1970s it was not the PCI, but groups to its left, such as *Lotta Continua* and *Autonomia*, that appeared most successful in mobilising young, radical workers.

Nevertheless, the PCI did benefit from a groundswell of support in the first half of the 1970s. This stemmed mainly from the new confidence of organised labour based on the *Statuto dei Lavoratori*, which conceded extensive rights to unskilled as well as skilled workers; but also from the radicalisation of youth. The party leadership responded with the strategy of the 'historic compromise' in 1973, aimed at broadening its appeal among the Catholic masses. After advances at local elections in 1975, this strategy was adapted to include the possibility of the PCI joining the ruling Christian Democrats in a government of 'national unity'. Following the 1976 national elections, when for the first time the party obtained over 30 per cent of the vote, the Christian Democrat government was forced to seek the PCI's support in parliament in order to continue in office. 'Though not in government', a commentator observes, 'the PCI seemed to have become a party of government.'[16]

For the PCI, the government of national unity between 1976 and 1979 was a disaster. First – faced with the most serious economic crisis of the post-war period – the government sought to impose an austerity programme, in which wage restraint and public-sector cuts were demanded of organised labour, in an attempt to restrict unemployment and maintain living standards. The Christian Democrat leadership thought it essential to bring the PCI into government, in order for the austerity programme to succeed. In the circumstances, all the PCI could do was to moderate the harsher elements of the programme. But it was none the less inevitable that the party should seem to be collaborating in the subjugation of organised labour and the working class.

At the same time, the upsurge of terrorism, culminating in the murder of the Christian Democrat Aldo Moro in March 1978, forced the PCI to appear as the defender of a State that was widely perceived as both oppressive and corrupt. It was significant that the Red Brigades' target in killing Moro was not the Christian Democrats, but the PCI and the 'historic compromise'. Far from achieving respectability from the experience of the government of national unity, the PCI had merely succeeded in identifying itself with a discredited state apparatus, and in alienating vital sections of the youth and working-class movements. As a leading member of the *Il Manifesto* group put it, '1976–79 was one of the worst periods of Italian history from which all the tragedies have stemmed.'[17]

The immediate consequence was the break-up of the informal alliance with the Christian Democrats, and the PCI's defeat at the 1979 elections. The longer-term effect was to open the way for a compact between the Christian Democrats and Craxi's remodelled Socialist Party, which produced one of the most right-wing administrations in Italy since the war. Despite a shift in PCI strategy after 1980, when the party called for an alliance of left-wing parties in a 'democratic alternative', no such coalition has been achieved. Meanwhile, it has suffered a steady decline in support at each subsequent election.

****

By the early 1980s, then, a number of Western Europe's major left-wing parties were in trouble. Programmes to tackle the capitalist recession that hit all the Western economies after 1973 had been unable to stem the rising tide of inflation and unemployment. In each case, conventional Keynesian reflationary remedies were gradually supplanted by more restrictive orthodox economic policies aimed at holding down wages and cutting public expenditure. To counter the social effects of the crisis, left-wing governments attempted to take punitive action against both industrial militancy and political terrorism. In the process parties such as Labour, the SPD and the PCI lost not only their traditional hold over the working class, but any vestigial claim to represent the forces of radicalism and change.

The quandary in which such parties found themselves by the late 1970s, however, was not merely the result of the prevailing social and economic conjuncture, but of their analagous development over the previous three decades and more. Seeking to approximate ever more closely to a consensus which they had only partly served to carve out, they became increasingly identified with that consensus, defined as the 'social democratic order'. The crisis of the 1970s succeeded in each case in only reinforcing the association. By the time the consensus began to crumble, therefore, it was the parties of the left that had come to stand for the 'established order' in its dotage. Radicalism had become the preserve of the parties of the right.

Outside a small circle of left-wing intellectuals, the depth of this political and ideological impasse was scarcely recognised at the time, least of all among the leaderships of the parties concerned. The electoral defeats of the late 1970s and early 1980s were softened by the reassuring hope that within a few years the political pendulum would swing inexorably back in their favour. Moreover, the more internationally aware could point to the accession of socialist parties to power in France, Spain, Italy and Greece. In the event such comfortable optimism has proved disconcertingly wide of the mark. For not only have the traditional parties of labour remained out of power ever since; the performance of the 'new socialist' parties in government has also revealed just how far to the right the political consensus has shifted in the 1980s.

The New Socialist Parties in the 1980s

Southern Europe

In contrast to the traditional parties of labour, the 'new socialist' parties which came to power in the late 1970s and early 1980s seemed to offer an innovative and rejuvenating radicalism. To begin with, they were based not in the old industrial heartlands of northern Europe, but in France and the Mediterranean south: Italy, Spain, Portugal and Greece. Their accession to power was accompanied in many cases by popular mobilisation on a scale not seen in Europe since the 1930s. In the last three states this was associated with the ending of a long period of right-wing dictatorship. In addition, they promised a fresh approach to socialism, which would go beyond the traditional formula of the mixed economy and the welfare state, towards new forms of social and economic democracy.

The new socialist parties in office did, in the event, mark a departure from the traditional social democracy of the north; but hardly in the ways anticipated. Far from expanding the socialist project into the 1980s, they took the regressive pragmatism of the 1970s a stage further. Rather than anticipating or paving the way for the drastic remedies of the New Conservatism, the new socialist governments pre-empted them: by implementing the same right-wing measures themselves. Their legacy has been to empty socialism of any radical content, to sever all that remains of its historical identification with the emancipation and empowerment of the working class – indeed, with any form of emancipation at all. The final ironic act in the lengthy drama of West European social democracy, it appears, is its transformation into the vanguard of the New Conservatism.

The most influential proponents of this shift have been the socialist administrations in France and Spain. Both the parties concerned, the *Parti Socialiste* (PS) and the *Partido Socialista Obrero Español* (PSOE), had a revered place within the history of the international socialist movement. Their significance in government was underlined by the obvious political and economic importance of their states within Western Europe.

Furthermore, both socialist administrations held overall parliamentary majorities, which meant that their programmes could proceed uncompromised by alliances or concessions. Their accession to power in the early 1980s consequently prompted a heightened interest. They seemed to offer the possibility of alternative approaches to questions of economic strategy and democracy, at a time when politics elsewhere in Europe was exhibiting a sharp rightward turn.

To call the socialist parties in France and Spain 'new' is, of course, something of a misnomer. While the origins of the French socialist tradition can be traced back to the 1789 Revolution, the PSOE had played a leading role in the development of Spanish socialism during the inter-war period, and in the Civil War of 1936–9. But in a specific sense both parties were new. Since 1945 the PSOE had been officially in exile; when it was reconstituted in Spain after Franco's dictatorship ended in 1975, it was under the leadership of a younger generation of socialists, like the future Prime Minister Felipe González, many of whom were not even born when Franco took power. In France, the socialists underwent a similar process: with the dissolution of the discredited SFIO in the late 1960s, and its re-foundation as the *Nouveau Parti Socialiste* between 1969 and 1972. In both cases the reconstruction of the parties signalled more than simply a change of name or leadership. It also involved a change of strategy and policy.

The French Socialists

By the late 1960s the French Socialist Party had reached a low ebb. At the 1969 presidential elections its candidate received only 5 per cent of the vote. When the party re-emerged in 1972 under the leadership of Mitterrand, therefore, it was with a new programme advocating an extension of public ownership and workers' control (*autogestion*), together with an important measure of administrative decentralisation. These policies were taken into the new strategic alliance with the Communist party (the *Union de la Gauche*), and incorporated into its *programme commun*. Thus in just three years, the PS underwent a substantial radicalisation, adopting many of the political themes developed in 1968. At the same time it attached its fortunes to those of the Communists, the predominant force on the French left in the early 1970s, who were capable of mobilising between 20 and 30 per cent of the vote.

The strategy was rapidly successful. During the 1970s the PS came to match – and eventually surpass – the Communist Party (PCF) in electoral popularity. The Communists' flirtation with Eurocommunism in the mid-1970s did nothing to curb the challenge to their ascendancy on the French left from the PS. The more the political identities of the parties appeared to merge, the more it was the Socialists alone who reaped the electoral benefits.

By 1978, the centre-right government's inability to mitigate the effects of economic depression presented the *Union de la Gauche* with a real opportunity for victory in that year's legislative elections. Fearing that a PS victory would place them in a subordinate position, however, the Communists abandoned the alliance; enabling Giscard d'Estaing's government to hold on to power. Yet by 1981, as the Socialists confirmed their electoral predominance on the left, Mitterrand was not only able to secure the presidency for himself, but to force the Communists back into an alliance for the legislative elections. In the event the alliance proved expendable, since the PS took office with an outright majority in parliament, though the Communist Party was granted four ministries – thus preserving the illusion of a coalition.

So the Socialists came to power in 1981 with a clear mandate for change, and no obstacles in the way of its enforcement. The right was divided and discredited after the failure of its economic policies; the Communists had been marginalised and subordinated to the PS. The party's programme, substantially unchanged from 1972 but reinforced by the *Projet socialiste* drawn up by the left after 1980, appeared radical. It seemed, moreover, as if the government was intent on implementing it.

In the first year of the administration, a number of large firms like Rhône-Poulenc were nationalised, industries such as mining were expanded, and the minimum wage and social security benefits were raised. A number of social reforms followed, including the lowering of the age of retirement, a reduction in the working week, the abolition of capital punishment, and an extension of workers' and women's rights. The government also sought to fulfil its commitment to decentralise the administrative process by giving greater powers to regional elected assemblies.

Yet within 12 months of taking office the socialist government made a spectacular *volte-face*, reversing previous policies and deploying instead the panoply of neo-liberal economic panaceas hitherto identified with the conservative regimes of Thatcher and Reagan. There were a number of reasons for this sudden about-turn. First, the government's expansionist programme precipitated panic in the financial markets, a rapid outflow of capital and an equally rapid decline in the value of the franc. Coupled with a rise in imports and the rate of inflation, which threatened living standards, the government faced an economic situation demanding remedial action, if hardly a reversal of strategy.

This predicament compounded the innate conservatism of a leadership which had never taken seriously the *Projet socialiste* of the party's left. Radical rhetoric was a useful electoral tool in emphasising party differences and projecting a dynamic and progressive image, but the leadership never confused it with radical practice. After 1981 the assertive party slogan, *change de société*, was dropped, and replaced by the altogether more bland appeal of *la force tranquille*, which Mitterrand was to prefer in his presidential campaign.[18]

Nevertheless, when the U-turn came after 1982, it ushered in a phase of policy-making more emphatically conservative than anything yet seen from a government of the left. Rather than merely seeking to enforce wage restraint, the government went a step further: it broke the wage-price index-link, effecting at a stroke what earlier conservative administrations had never dared to do. Subsidies to nationalised industries were cut back, and management was given a free hand to undertake extensive redundancy programmes: 500,000 jobs were to go in major sectors such as coal, steel and transport. In the four years of Socialist office after 1982, unemployment rose by over 30 per cent to almost 2.5 million.

These measures in turn seriously undermined the position of organised labour, reducing the trade unions' bargaining power and their ability to defend workers against wage cuts and job losses. The government led the way in encouraging an aggressive approach to labour relations: having reneged on its commitment to expand the mining industry, it was prepared to used armed police to defeat a series of bitter miners' strikes.

At the same time as it sought to reduce the costs and power of labour, the Mitterrand administration was actively aiming to increase the scope and profitability of capital on the 'open economy' model. Income tax was cut, exchange controls loosened, and the Paris Bourse liberalised, by opening markets to foreign competition, thus sparking off a financial boom. The first moves to privatisation were initiated after 1984 by the Finance Minister Pierre Bérégovoy, who envisaged selling off parts of the public sector as a means to reduce government debts.

By this stage it was clear that the Socialist leadership thought business functioned most efficiently as capitalist enterprise. By 1986 it was possible for the right-wing business journal *The Economist* to pronounce wryly that 'after five years of socialist government, France is in some ways a better specimen of capitalism than before.'[19] From the opposite end of the political spectrum a shrewd observer, Daniel Singer, came to a similar conclusion. Left and right in France were now speaking an identical language: 'they are partners in the same system, no longer proponents of contrasting societies.'[20]

An equally conservative emphasis was evident in both defence policy and party management. The once vocal anti-nuclear lobby was silenced as in Gaullist style the leadership upheld France's *force de frappe*, outstripping the right in its support for the US decision to site a fresh generation of NATO missiles in Western Europe. Steps were taken to prevent the voicing of opposition to government policy, inside or outside the party. Mitterrand, the Prime Minister Mauroy and the party leader Jospin met weekly to discuss ways of keeping the parliamentary party in check and the rank-and-file submissive.[21] The presence of Communists in the government was used to stifle labour protest – through their close relationship with the *Confédération Général du Travail* (CGT) – though the high level of unemployment was undoubtedly the most effective means of disciplining unions and constraining militancy.

Dominating this hastily constructed edifice of abeyance and compromise was the increasingly autocratic figure of Mitterrand, the most powerful and authoritarian president since de Gaulle.

But the necessity of 'crisis management' and the pragmatic nature of the Socialist leadership in France do not fully account for the Mitterrand administration's shift in policy after 1982. It actually marked a new, and more extreme, departure from the kind of policy pursued by Europe's social democratic governments in the late 1970s. Though the administration was quick to dissociate its policies from the forms of economic liberalism identified with the Reagan and Thatcher governments, they were none the less comparable in intention and effect.

The fundamental aim was to restructure capital – above all big capital – by opening the economy to international market forces, making labour more 'flexible', and wages more 'responsive' to the needs of capital investment; and thus creating the internal conditions for more profitable capital accumulation. Such priorities could hardly be admitted in public, but their outline was increasingly evident in Mitterrand's impatient rejoinders to the criticisms of the left: 'When it has been explained to me how to distribute what we are not producing and how to win markets, starting at home, with industries twenty years behind their competitors, I may start being interested.'[22]

Behind this exasperated expression of apparent common sense lay a far more regressive project to restore capitalist enterprise at the expense of social needs. The Mitterrand government not only jettisoned its former commitment to active state intervention and embraced the model of market-led modernisation, but it was also clearly prepared to make the French working class bear the full brunt of the process.

It was not surprising, therefore, that the government's popularity fell drastically in the aftermath of its conversion to free-market economics, or that its favouring of large over small capital, and the private over the public sector, alienated small business and white-collar workers as well as manual labour. In the face of the remarkable subordination of government policy to the demands of private capital, those social reforms that were passed seemed small consolation. In France the Socialists did not simply pave the way to the New Conservatism of the Chirac government, they set it in motion.

The Spanish Socialists

But the most spectacular instance of socialist apostasy, the surreptitious slippage towards a politics of the right, has come from the Spanish Socialist government of Felipe González since 1982. Like the French PS, the PSOE was revived in the 1970s, though here, it was the result of the end of the Franco dictatorship and the restoration of political democracy.

In fact, the PSOE re-emerged after 1975 with its radical reputation intact, and it was buoyed by the wave of popular enthusiasm for democracy. At its Congress in 1976 the party affirmed its credentials as 'a class party with a mass character, Marxist and democratic', committed to the 'taking of political and economic power, the socialisation of the means of production, distribution and exchange by the working class'.[23] Such rhetoric appeared startlingly uncompromising in the climate of accommodation that had pervaded European socialist politics since Bad Godesberg.

Mere rhetoric, it was, however, directed by the need to sever connections with the previous dictatorship and to give vent to the radical sentiment and industrial militancy that accompanied the passing of the old order. The leadership, including González and his close associate Alfonso Guerra, had never shown the slightest intention of taking the party down the road of Marxist-inspired social transformation.

Their initial aim was to mould the PSOE into a social democratic party on Western European lines, as exemplified by the German SPD. Thus when Alfredo Suárez, a moderate conservative, was appointed to oversee the transition to parliamentary democracy in 1976, the party gave active support. It conceded an electoral system weighted in favour of the more traditionally right-wing rural areas, and helped to lay down the liberal constitution of 1978. Most significant, the Socialists, together with the Communist Party (*Partido Comunista de España* – PCE), consented to the Moncloa Pact of 1977, a form of 'social contract' drawn up by Suárez and the ruling conservative *Unión de Centro Democrático* (UCD), in which welfare reforms were promised in return for wage restraint. What previously had been the most militant and class-conscious labour movement in Western Europe was consequently subordinated to a strategy of political accommodation.

But the real turning-point for the PSOE came after its defeat by Suárez and the UCD at the 1979 elections. At the 1979 party congress, González and the leadership called for a decisive break with the PSOE's Marxist inheritance. A bitter struggle ensued in which González, backed by the moral and financial weight of the German SPD and Socialist International, emerged victorious only after threatening to resign. Marxists were purged from the party executive, and a section of the left withdrawn from its ranks.

From here events played into the hands of the moderate PSOE leaders. On the left, the Communist PCE self-destructed as a result of the Moncloa compromise, internal faction-fighting and successive electoral disappointments. On the right, the governing UCD coalition collapsed, as the sharp differences between its numerous political components were exposed once it had fulfilled its task of installing parliamentary democracy. The traditional Catholic conservatives had been discredited by the Civil Guard's attempted coup in February 1981. At the same time, social democratic forces within the coalition deserted Suárez and merged with the newly deradicalised Socialists.

By the time of the elections in October 1982 there was in Spain no serious opposition to the PSOE. Consequently, victory gave the PSOE the second largest parliamentary majority ever achieved by a West European socialist party.

Two points were of special significance in this breakthrough. First, the PSOE came to power in 1982 without any mass mobilisation of support. Its victory owed as much to the disintegration of the other parties as to its own efforts, a verdict affirmed by the fact that the party membership actually declined over the two years before the election. Second, in contrast with the Socialist Party in France in 1981, the PSOE entered government without any clear-cut programme. Its major commitments were simply to halve the numbers of unemployed and to introduce a referendum on the question of NATO, which Spain had joined in 1981. Policies involving nationalisation and state intervention in the economy were identified less with the PSOE, than with Suárez's new moderate *Centro Democrático Y Social* (CDS), which could, by now, legitimately claim to represent a political force to the left of the Socialists.

Once in government, however, the PSOE consolidated its rightward shift in economic, social and foreign policy. Government strategy was directed towards restructuring the Spanish economy to facilitate its insertion into the international market economy, and to prepare specifically for entry into the EC.

In practice this meant a series of policies similar to – and in some cases more regressive than – those of the Mitterrand administration after 1982. Employers were directly aided by cuts in income and corporation tax, and reductions in their national insurance contributions. A privatisation drive began, aimed at selling profitable parts of large state-owned concerns like the *Instituto*

Nacional de Industría (INI). Inflation was tackled by severe austerity measures aimed at reducing government expenditure and enforcing wage restraint on organised labour. Finally, the labour market was itself 'streamlined' and rendered more 'flexible' by a programme of compulsory redundancies in state industries, and by diminishing job security with the introduction of a system of six-monthly contracts in key areas of employment. Here Socialists were to be seen unabashedly clearing the ground for the systematic operation of market forces.

By contrast, most of the widely heralded social reforms were more cosmetic than real. The 1983 abortion law, for example, projected internationally as a body-blow to traditional Catholic fundamentalism, was highly restrictive in practice. In 1985 it was possible for a representative of the women's movement to assert that 'no woman has yet had a legal abortion in Spain.'[24] Divorce was legalised in 1981 under the Suárez government, but again no attempts were made by the Socialist administration to monitor its working, to liberalise its interpretation, or prevent the widespread evasion of alimony payments. Plans to extend education and welfare foundered on the lack of funds caused by the government's spending cuts.

The absence of commitment to much-needed public reform appears all the more stark when compared with the massive investment made in the military. After the Socialists took office in 1982, military expenditure rose faster than under the Franco regime. During the same period, the PSOE leadership steadily withdrew its former opposition to NATO and, like Mitterrand in France, extended support to the siting of Cruise and Pershing missiles in Western Europe. Unlike the French Socialists, however, the PSOE was pledged to a referendum on NATO membership from which it could not retreat. In the campaign that followed, the Socialist government did not act as a neutral arbiter. It deployed the considerable resources of the State, including a mass advertising campaign costing over $5 million, to persuade the electorate of the indispensability of membership. The contest proved to be the Socialists' stiffest test yet, and victory the high-water mark of their increasingly centralist and dictatorial style of government.

Shortly afterwards, at the general election of June 1986, the PSOE won a second term of office, despite a marked decline in its vote, which was largely due to continuing divisions on both left and right. The party had confirmed its status as the consolidator of parliamentary democracy, the representative of economic and military modernisation – in short, as the new face of conservatism in Spain.

Since 1985, opposition to the González regime has steadily mounted. The government's economic policies, and above all its cynical disregard for electoral promises to reduce unemployment, have angered the labour movement. Far from diminishing, the official rate of unemployment rose from 17 per cent in 1982 to 22 per cent in 1985, and has remained over 20 per cent since – by far the highest rate nationally in Western Europe. 1985 saw an unprecedented denunciation of the government's economic programme by the leader of the PSOE-affiliated *Unión General de Trabajadores* (UGT) and former González ally, Nicolás Redondo:

> What is certain is that this version of market economy, which is presented to us as the only one possible and the universal panacea, is bringing to our country nothing other than greater unemployment, greater inequality and greater poverty.[25]

Entry into the EC in 1986, proclaimed by the government as its greatest achievement, has brought labour only further problems, hitting both agriculture and industry: Spain's main lines of production, from wine and olive oil to steel and cars, are those in which the Community already has a surfeit.

By 1987, therefore, the PSOE administration faced massive protests organised by the UGT and the resurgent Communist unions, *Comisiones Obreras*: against job losses, its 5 per cent ceiling on wage increases, and the whole conservative thrust of economic policy. Labour, it seemed, was no longer prepared to countenance a programme of modernisation carried out in the name of socialism. As Redondo forcibly expressed it: 'The government stands legitimately accused of doing little that bears any ostensible relevance to the cause of socialism or the working class.'[26] The mass disaffection of labour has been paralleled by a growth in opposition among other groups -- notably youth, which have been the prime victims of high unemployment – but also among teachers and public-sector workers hit by cuts in state spending.

The increasingly authoritarian style of González and Guerra has also attracted voluble criticism. The cynical manipulation of the democratic process in the NATO referendum was a notably artless example. But since 1986, González has shown equal contempt for the *Cortes* as a democratic forum, making only one parliamentary appearance in the seven months after the election. His treatment of the popular protest against government measures has been similarly dismissive: in April 1987 he declared himself not 'particularly overwhelmed'.[27]

Unsurprisingly, the PSOE lost over a million votes at the local and European elections, while its affiliated membership has sunk to the lowest, proportionate to electoral strength, of any major party of left or right in Europe. Its faltering ascendancy in Spain has come to depend largely on a divided opposition, the debilitated state of organised labour under high levels of unemployment, and the leadership's capacity to convince a majority that there are no alternative remedies to its own stringent prescriptions. Within the space of ten years, the PSOE under González and Guerra has completed a remarkable transformation, from the most radical to the most conservative socialist party in Western Europe.

* * * *

The experiences of socialist government in France and Spain are by no means exceptional in the 1980s. The forms of conservative politics pursued under Mitterrand and González can be discerned more widely in states of southern Europe where socialists have held power. The economic policies developed under Craxi in Italy after 1983, such as the gradual dismantling of the *scala mobile* whereby wage levels were linked to inflation, have obvious parallels. So too do the privatisation initiatives and the cuts in public expenditure undertaken by the second Soares administration in Portugal during the early 1980s. Likewise in Greece, the calls for a general strike in 1987, in opposition to the Panhellenic Socialist Movement (PASOK) administration's austerity programme, bear direct comparison with the political situation prevailing at the same time in Spain. The examples could be elaborated and multiplied, but the process would only reiterate the pattern already indicated. What remains to be clarified, rather, is the importance of the pattern itself, its significance within the evolving configuration of Western politics.

The basic pattern of economic development pursued by socialist administrations in the 1980s has been one of export-oriented growth generated by private enterprise. Socialist governments have assisted in this process by helping to create the conditions for more profitable capital accumulation: 'supply-side' incentives in the form of tax relief for business, austerity measures to reduce labour costs, cuts in public expenditure to lower inflation. Their main function has been to foster the 'restructuring' of national capital, to facilitate the extension of links between national capital and the international economy, and to enable it to compete within international markets.

The form in which this task presented itself was determined by the timing of the socialist parties' accession to power: in France, Italy, Spain, Portugal and Greece alike, they took office at a period of capitalist recession. Moreover, in almost all cases parties of the right, who might have been expected to carry through the task, were unfit for it. In Spain, Portugal and Greece, the right was associated with traditionalist dictatorships, whose incapacity to bring about social and economic modernisation had been one of the major reasons for their ultimate collapse. In Italy, the Christian Democrats were an unsuitable vehicle for modernisation, due to their identification with Catholic traditionalism and the legacy of post-war statism. A brief flirtation with a 'modernising' image in 1983 had proved electorally disastrous. In France the right was discredited by its handling of economic recession in the 1970s. It was thus not only feasible, but from the point of view of the established order in the respective states, politically essential, that the socialist parties should be cast as the saviours of domestic capital.

The conservative nature of the 'new socialism' was further enhanced by the bureaucratic character of the leadership and party cadres. The mass mobilisation that accompanied the revival of socialist parties in the 1970s did not bring forward popular leaders closely linked to the rank-and-file of the labour movement. Instead, the groundswell of mass support was merely used by the party leaderships, technocratic by training and outlook, to establish themselves in the pre-existing state apparatus and develop close ties with the key institutions of the international financial order, the IMF and the World Bank.

The socialist parties were used in turn as a vehicle of advancement by young middle-class technocrats, who were more attuned to the prevailing international economic orthodoxy than to any indigenous or alternative model of development. Both socially and ideologically, the political class that staffed the socialist administrations of the 1980s was far removed from the labour movement and working class. Its links were habitually best developed with the domestic industrial, financial and administrative elites, and with the cosmopolitan technocracy of the new international monetary order. Not surprisingly, therefore, it absorbed the dominant economic logic of these groups, which by the early 1980s was turning inexorably towards a markedly anti-statist neo-liberalism.

However one tries to explain the conduct of socialist parties in office during the 1980s, its significance is clear enough. The version of post-war social democracy that combines selective economic intervention with welfarism may show a diminished understanding of the possibilities of socialist transformation. But what is striking about the 'new socialism' is its abandonment of any kind of transforming vision – except for that formulated by the right. The collective apostasy of socialist parties in the 1980s has resulted, in the words of James Petras, in nothing less than:

> [an] historic shift to neo-liberal orthodoxy, which has pulled the whole political debate further to the right and has set up a situation in which what remains of the left is the sole 'conservative' force in the generic sense of the term – the only group defending the existing standard of living, the importance of state-owned enterprises for national development, the treatment of labour as something other than a commodity.[28]

The effects of this shift have been profoundly damaging. In countries such as Spain, Portugal and Greece where the welfare system remains relatively rudimentary, and wages low, the high levels of unemployment and reductions in public spending stemming from government policy have had predictably dire repercussions on the poorer sections of the population. Nor is this situation likely to improve on entry into the EC and increased exposure to world markets. The major impact of these moves has already been to push down labour costs and reinforce the historical subordination of these countries' economies within the international division of labour.

But the price to be paid is not only economic. In weighting their policies so heavily in favour of capital, parties like the Spanish PSOE have managed to forge a decisive rupture in their relationship with labour organisations and with the working class. Most costly of all, however, has been the devaluation of socialism as a political ideology capable of materially benefitting and empowering working-class men and women. In the end, it may be this that represents the true measure of the right's revolution in the 1980s.

Unions, Movements and Parties

For over a century, the development of socialism in Europe has been based on an alliance between socialist parties and trade unions, the 'labour movement'; and between these and other progressive extra-parliamentary associations such as the anti-fascist or the cooperative movement. In practice, the unity has consistently been less than total, but it has never been seriously displaced as the necessary foundation for an effective socialist movement. Yet since the 1970s the inter-relationship of unions, party and movements has seemed increasingly fragile. The natural confluence of interest has come to be questioned under the combined impact of declining trade-union power, electoral defeat and the emergence of a 'post-materialist' politics. Trade unions, socialist parties and social movements have seemed as much a liability to each other as a source of mutual strength.

The Trade Unions

The difficulties of the trade unions were relatively recent and sudden. In the period 1968–74, unions in France, Italy, Britain, West Germany and Spain undertook major waves of industrial strikes, altogether unexpected in their scale and militancy. The results were a series of legal and material advances for workers, a recognition of their growth in power within these states, and new peaks in union membership.

After 1974, when international economic recession brought with it unemployment on a scale not seen since the 1930s, these gains in rights, economic power and membership were rapidly eroded. Unions were forced to accept wage cuts, or more 'flexible' working practices and massive lay-offs. In the steel industry, for example, the workforce was cut by anything between one-third and one-half in the decade after 1975 in Italy, Belgium, West Germany, France and Britain.[29] Trade-union membership fell heavily: in Britain the total declined from 13 million to 10 million between 1979 and 1986; in Spain the membership of the UGT halved from 1.4 million to 700,000 between 1982 and 1986.[30] By the mid-1980s, nowhere in Western Europe was the situation better than stable, and there were also signs of longer-term problems in a widespread failure to recruit among the young.

The recession, accompanied by employer and government offensives, did more than reverse earlier advances. It exposed the inherent weaknesses of trades-unionism in relation to both capital and the State. These weaknesses were revealed most starkly in the case of the traditionally powerful unions in heavy industries: steel, coal and shipbuilding, for example. There were important differences in the role and organisation of unions in these industries across the continent, but the common factors in their decline in the decade after 1974 were none the less significant.

First, divisions were increasingly evident between moderates and militants, leadership and rank-and-file, but also between unions on the basis of political, religious or ideological differences. Second, unions found it difficult to make their presence count politically. Where governments of left or right sought to 'rationalise' industries after 1980, the institutional framework of tripartite decision-making was either abandoned, as in France and Britain, or seriously weakened, as in Belgium and West Germany. Indeed, outside Italy and West Germany – where worker participation had been enshrined in the *Carta dei Lavoratori* and the system of *Mitbestimmung* – the unions' lack of effective influence over decision-making, at either the industrial or political level, was woefully exposed.

This points to a further fundamental weakness in the trade-union movement: the lack of a viable alternative strategy to that of management. With their essentially defensive or 'economistic' outlook, unions tended to respond to capitalist recession and restructuring either by calls for protectionism and maintained capacity for a product that was already over-supplied, or as in the case of West German unions like *IG Metall*, by accepting the need for modernisation and trying to limit the social damage. All too often, unions failed to grasp the structural nature of the crisis in the 1970s, and therefore concentrated on preserving the status quo, while waiting for the anticipated revival of demand. In the absence of strategic initiative or foresight the unions were forced either to engage in a series of bitter and fruitless strikes, or to acquiesce in the 'rationalisation' of production.

The case of the unions in Scandinavia may seem to lie outside this scenario, yet even in Sweden the Wage Earner Funds scheme of the 1970s, which envisaged a major extension of labour's power through a system of collective share-ownership, was never implemented.[31] Since the mid-1980s the Swedish unions have been no less on the defensive than their counterparts elsewhere.

Throughout Western Europe, union power has been further eroded in the 1980s by conservative legislation (see Chapter 2) and, more fundamentally, by changes in the structure of capital and the conduct of management. Unions have made little headway in the new, advanced sectors, like information technology, which have come to represent the leading edge of the 'enterprise culture'. New styles of management have succeeded in bypassing union structures, dealing directly with workers conceived as a 'human resource', whose productivity is maximised through material incentives and the skilful use of industrial psychology.

Under pressure from all sides, the unions have adapted their tactics and demands to the more bracing climate of the times. The widely noted mood of 'new realism' among labour organisations was evident everywhere in Western Europe, including Scandinavia, by the mid-1980s. Unions in Scandinavia had ceased to press for an extension of workers' rights. In West Germany, formerly militant industrial unions like *IG Metall* opposed factory occupation as a means of protesting against lay-offs or the closure of plants. Throughout Belgium, the Netherlands and West Germany, labour organisations concentrated their efforts on obtaining shorter working hours rather than wage increases. Schemes to extend worker participation in industry, which had been enthusiastically forwarded in the later 1970s in Britain, France and West Germany as well as in Sweden, were quietly shelved and forgotten.

Strains have also developed in the relationship between unions and their traditional allies, the labour parties. They were evident in the attempts by the Labour Party in Britain and the PCI in Italy to maintain the 'social contract' between government and organised working class in the 1970s, and have become even more marked under the 'austerity programmes' of the southern European socialist administrations of the 1980s. Increasingly, the historical understanding between parties and key unions has been used instrumentally by governments of the left to underwrite their deflationary and wage-restrictive policies. In countries like Spain, Portugal and Italy, trade unions have come to be seen by socialist politicians as 'transmission belts' of state policy, and watchdogs over working-class recalcitrance.

In northern Europe where socialists are out of office, parties of the left continue to act formally as the 'political attorneys' of the unions. On occasions, this can create a powerful bloc of opposition to New Conservative policy – as in the mass protest of the West German labour movement against the Kohl government's attempt to restrict the right to strike in 1985. But it has been more characteristic in the 1980s to witness the efforts of left parties to distance themselves from the most critical struggles of organised labour. A notable example was the evasive conduct of the British Labour Party in the miners' strike of 1984–5.

At the same time, the trade unions in Western Europe can hardly be seen as a radical force in the 1980s. More often they have acted as a conservative influence on socialist parties. The West German unions sided with the pro-nuclear lobby in the debates within the SPD over NATO missiles in the early 1980s. They have continued to face allegations of racism, on grounds that they allow immigrant workers to bear the brunt of lay-offs in order to preserve the jobs of their 'core membership'. Such practices, the unions allege, are part of a wider union strategy to distinguish between 'sheltered' and 'non-sheltered' fractions of the working class, with the aim of protecting the former at the expense of the latter.[32]

But whether such allegations against the trade unions have substance or not, they point to a more general criticism of unions from the left in the 1980s: that they are fundamentally conservative organisations that serve, primarily, the interests of the white, male, skilled worker. By extension, it has become possible to ask whether the formal ties between party and trade-union movement are now anything more than an historical anachronism. The renunciation of these ties, it is argued, would allow socialist parties to broaden their appeal to social constituencies beyond the dwindling communities of the industrial working class, while the unions in turn would be freed from outmoded political allegiances, to attend more closely to the needs of their members.[33]

The Social Movements

The acceptance of such arguments on the left suggests how far the break-up of the inherited formations of socialism has already come. Much of the impulse for the critique of the old-style labour movement has come from forces outside its ambit, yet still undisputably part of the left. It was no mere coincidence that the years that saw the last great upsurge of labour militancy after 1968 also witnessed the emergence of new social movements: feminism, ecology, anti-racism. The growth of these movements characteristically occurred outside the traditional institutions of labour, whether these be party or trade unions.

Indeed, a number of the movements, like the West German Greens or the Italian *Autonomia*, derived much of their radical impulse from a rejection of established labour institutions, which they saw as irredeemably compromised with the existing political order. The rapid evaporation of industrial militancy after 1974 and the return to power of socialist governments firmly wedded to reformism, only confirmed a widespread belief among radicalised youth that the old organisations of the working class had become a part of the problem, not a means to its solution.

What has been significant about the development of the new social movements is, first, their spread throughout Western Europe since the early 1970s. The impact of the women's, green and peace movements has been very widely registered, from the states of the Mediterranean south to Scandinavia. Naturally, the configuration and relative strength of particular movements varies between countries. West Germany has become prototypical, though by no means exceptional, for the way in which environmental and peace issues became embodied within its political system through the Green Party. Italy has been conspicuous as the home of one of the West's most powerful feminist movements. Britain was notable in the 1970s for the effective mobilisation of popular opposition to racism, through the Anti-Nazi League. The only possible exception to the general pattern is France, where such movements have had a curiously low profile.[34]

In addition, the new social movements have highlighted the proliferation of sources of social conflict beyond the industrial workplace and party meeting. They have brought questions of gender, race, militarism and environment from the margins to the centre of political debate. By the mid-1980s it was becoming increasingly difficult for the old-established left to dismiss these as minority or 'lifestyle' issues.

Feminism has been fundamentally concerned not merely with male dominance in the abstract, but with its embodiment in the unequal distribution of power and resources in society – a 'knife and fork' question of the first order. The ecological movement which grew up in Dutch and West German cities in the later 1970s was shaped as much by issues of housing, as by nuclear power. Or again, the cultural policies developed by socialists at the municipal level in Italy and Britain have had considerable bearing on problems of urban employment and law and order. Successful cultural services and industries stimulate both direct and indirect employment, while the encouragement of an active urban nightlife is one known means to reduce the threat of rape and violent crime, which thrive on lifeless and deserted streets.[35]

Nevertheless, relations between the new social movements and the traditional organisations of the left have been at best ambivalent. The former were generated autonomously, often in active opposition to the existing socialist parties and labour movement, and they continued to develop through the 1970s in an atmosphere of mutual suspicion. It was characteristic that when the West German Greens emerged as a coherent political entity after 1980, they defined themselves as an 'anti-party party', in deliberate contrast with the SPD, as well as the parties of the centre and right.

Conversely, the antipathy of the established labour organisations to the new social movements has frequently been marked. Prior to 1982, leading sections of the PCI and the SPD, as well as the bulk of the Italian and West German trade unions, remained critical of the peace movement. In Spain, the subsequent vice-president of the

Socialist PSOE, Alfonso Guerra, expressed the party leadership's hostility to the growing women's movement in 1978 by publicly labelling it 'absolutely reactionary'.[36] In this climate of mistrust, the peace movement in particular developed its closest links not with the political or industrial representatives of labour, but with other independent or voluntary groups. Most notable were church organisations: the Inter-Church Peace Council (IKV) in the Netherlands and the Protestant churches in West Germany, were both instrumental in orchestrating disarmament campaigns, as were similar religious associations in Britain and Spain.

The issues raised by the new social movements, however, have continued to permeate a wider political culture in the 1980s; and this has forced the labour movement as a whole, and socialist parties in particular, to adopt a more positive attitude. The extent to which the major European parties of the left have been prepared to align themselves with the new movements, or incorporate new issues within their programmes, has depended on the degree of electoral threat that these pose, as well as on the responsiveness of the parties themselves. It is not coincidental that the process of realignment has been most advanced in West Germany, where the SPD has faced growing electoral competition from the Greens since 1983; and in Italy where several parties, like the Socialists and the Radicals, bid alongside the PCI for the votes of the social movements.

In West Germany the attempt to reconcile the SPD with the 'new politics' was inaugurated by Brandt and Peter Glotz, its general secretary, in 1983. The aim was to undercut support for the Greens by emphasising the party's progressive commitment on questions of the environment, nuclear power, women's rights and disarmament. Despite doubts and setbacks, the direction has been since extended, to incorporate further emphases on cultural policy and the 'new internationalism'. According to Glotz, these issues have provided the basis for a programmatic shift of equivalent significance to that achieved at Bad Godesberg.[37]

Similarly, the Italian PCI's adoption of the 'democratic alternative' strategy after 1980 acted as a catalyst for the party to align itself more closely with the powerful social forces that had remained distant from it in the 1970s. The 1983 election saw the left of the party making overtures to women, ecologists and gays, and to the peace movement, following the siting of Cruise missiles at Comiso, Sicily. By 1984 the PCI had begun to attract important elements of the social movements into its orbit, signalled by the return to the party fold of the *Il Manifesto* group and its political embodiment, the party of Proletarian Unity (PDUP). Like the West German SPD, therefore, the PCI entered the 1987 elections with its radical credentials renewed, a strongly 'pluralist' prospectus, and a legitimate claim to be the sole party capable of installing the 'new politics' at the centre of a programme of government.

However, the realignment of the left suggested by these tendencies has been neither evenly registered nor markedly successful. Neither of the parties that have most conspicuously embraced the 'new politics', the SPD and the PCI, have managed to regain office or to halt their electoral decline. Both have suffered a steady erosion of their electoral base in the industrial working class during the 1980s, which may have been accelerated by the turn to 'new politics'. They have simultaneously failed to stem the rise of support for green and 'single issue' parties, or to draw in new constituencies.

This in turn has resuscitated internal party divisions. The PCI became locked in a series of critical debates in the aftermath of its 1987 electoral defeat, with the party's right arguing for a reversal of the previous emphasis on 'marginal' groups such as gays and feminists, a return to a moderate and traditional reformist policies, and an alliance with the Socialists. The West German left in general, and the SPD in particular, has likewise been wracked by the problem of a 'Red-Green' coalition since 1985, which the contrasting fortunes of the parties at the 1987 elections only intensified. On the present evidence, therefore, it can only be said that the attempted marriage of the new social movements with the traditional parties of labour has proved a thorny and, as yet, largely unproductive union.

Local Initiatives

But thorns and all, outside West Germany and Italy this process of realignment has not proceeded at a commensurate pace. In Britain, initiatives to link the interests of the social movements with policy were undertaken, highly successfully, at the municipal level. For a brief period in the early 1980s, indeed, the Labour-led Greater London Council represented a model of how a popular radical politics could be constructed, combining innovative policies for local industry and urban transport with a commitment to groups conventionally ignored by political institutions: women, gays, ethnic communities.

Such imaginative idealism, however, was not shared by the Labour leadership at the national level. It shrank from identifying too closely with a politics generated outside the traditional ranks of trade-union and parliamentary labourism, and therefore did little to inhibit the abolition of the metropolitan councils by the Thatcher government in 1986. On issues like anti-racism and sexual politics, party officialdom has likewise been keen to keep a distance, to preserve a moderate, parliamentary 'respectability'. It was noticeable, for example, that the right-wing's attacks on 'loony left' councils during the 1987 election campaign went almost wholly unanswered by Labour leaders.

In France the Socialists have adopted a similar approach, seeking to project the party as the moderate and 'responsible' alternative to the right. Policies on race and women are thus presented as rational additions to a modest quota of social reform, rather than as the basis for a reordered vision of political change. The Spanish Socialist government has been largely disdainful of such movements, as witnessed by its vociferous opposition to the peace movement on the NATO question, and by a continued ambivalence towards women's issues. On the one hand it established an Institute of Women's Affairs as part of its modernisation programme; on the other it rejected an EC directive to promote women's employment.

****

Thus while in some parts of Western Europe the move to forge a 'new politics' is well advanced, elsewhere it has scarcely begun. What this underlines is how complex, intricate and protracted the task of constructing a new socialist politics is likely to be. It requires, in effect, a programmatic vision capable of welding the new, expansionary, yet often fragmented forms of political awareness, to the still powerful – if changing – class consciousness of labour.

The linkage might appear inherently problematic, given the impacted character of the labour movement in many West European states, and the superficially narrow and 'non-material' focus of the social movements. As Raymond Williams has observed, 'it is significant that the new movements are active and substantial in almost every area of life except ... the economy.'[38]

This lack of articulation between different elements of the left represents one of its major current weaknesses in almost all Western countries. It is evident even where a significant realignment of the left has taken place, in West Germany and Italy. One of the primary reasons for the recent electoral failures of the SPD and PCI was their attempt to act as a political umbrella for a multiplicity of grievances, without constructing out of these any convincing programmatic unity. Not the least of the left's problems is the fact that support for these issues does not automatically translate into support for parties of the left. As Eva Kolinsky points out, 'research into political orientations of young people has shown that new issues of opposition or political commitment are unlikely to change party preferences and normally exist alongside them.'[39] Constructing a new politics will take more than a simple appeal to an assortment of popular discontents.

Yet the resources for such a project are clearly present in Western Europe. Contrary to the views of more jaundiced and isolated observers, the 1980s have witnessed an explosion of political activity: mass demonstrations against austerity programmes and nuclear arms, against conservative reform of education and sexual rights, against racism, famine and apartheid. The numbers participating in these protests and celebrations encompass millions. In the face of such popular manifestations, and the scale and breadth of their concern, it is hard to doubt the spread of politicisation across Western Europe. As a member of a new generation of working-class rock bands archly remarked in 1985: 'You *have* to be interested in politics these days. If you are not, you are a completely lost individual.'[40]

The extension of sharpened forms of political consciousness into those spheres of social existence that are conventionally seen as devoid of political content, like sexual relations and popular culture, is one reason why the phenomenon can be overlooked by the political establishment, including by parties of the left. But until it can be more fully harnessed with the traditional concerns of class and labour politics, until politics itself can be more fully 'socialised', a renewal of socialism in Western Europe is unlikely to take place. The alternatives to this project for the left are bleak indeed: either a state of political stagnation, or a return to the calculative, technocratic and fundamentally conservative politics, as practised by nominally socialist parties in office in the 1980s – parties which have, to all intents and purposes, already collapsed into the arms of the right.

5

Conclusion:
The Shape of Politics to Come

In the late 1980s the politics I have called here the New
Conservatism has come to predominate in most states of Western
Europe. Its impact has not been everywhere the same. As my study
has sought to show, the conservatism of the 1980s has been
introduced under diverse political auspices, including those of
nominally socialist parties, and it has likewise been adapted to fit
the historically specific conditions of different states. 'Thatcherism'
does not serve as a precise model of the kinds of politics pursued
by governments in West Germany, Italy or Spain.

The New Consensus

The degree of correspondence between current government
policy-making in states across Western Europe is none the less
striking. It amounts to nothing short of a new consensus. This
uniformity has been forged in response to a common set of
international imperatives, evolving from the world economic
recession of the later 1970s and early 1980s and the attendant
restructuring of finance and industrial capital. Since the early
1980s, and in some cases before, almost all governments, whether
of left or right, have resorted to policies of economic
neo-liberalism. In northern Europe, parties of the right were the
first to benefit politically from the crisis. They rejected the
post-war inheritance of interventionist economic management and
actively sought to promote capital restructuring and the
profitability of business by a combination of monetarist controls
and supply-side incentives.

But European parties of the right have played a leading role in
developing this new economic consensus and projecting it
internationally. The British Foreign Minister, Sir Geoffrey Howe,
has spoken rosily of Europe as 'setting the agenda' economically in
a 'fascinating and breath-taking way', using 'the whole thrust of
liberal economics as a means of bringing wealth to the starving'.[1]

The right has similarly succeeded in reordering the agenda of
international institutions like the European Community. By 1986 it

was possible for the Community's own journal to announce a fundamental change in policy direction:

> A quiet revolution, virtually unobserved, is occurring in the European Community's strategy towards business ... For business the clearest indication of the sea-change in EC priorities is that policies that once were used to exert public control over multinational companies are now being deliberately used to free enterprises from legal obstacles to transnational activity ... From a corporate standpoint, the change is from a policy seeking to alter the balance of European industrial relations in favour of organised labour (and therefore a threat) to one seeking to help meet industry's training requirements (and thus a service).[2]

In these ways, the forces of the right have sought to align themselves with new developments in advanced capitalism – the internationalisation of finance and manufacturing, the trend to 'flexible accumulation', and so on. This deeper alignment has meant that right-wing parties came to be identified with the thrust to modernity, leaving the socialist parties and wider labour movement to appear the representatives of an increasingly vestigial industrial society.

The Socialists' Rightward Shift
In southern Europe, on the other hand, it has been socialist parties that have implemented equivalent neo-liberal economic measures. Here, nominally socialist parties present themselves as 'modernisers'. From this perspective, the alleged revival of social democracy in the late 1980s, which was heralded by the return to power of the Socialists in France and the break-up of right-wing coalitions in Belgium and the Netherlands, is in no sense the harbinger of real change. It is likely to represent nothing more than a continuation of the same politics in different guise. This ideological uniformity will receive its official rubber-stamp with the establishment of the European internal market in 1992. This will effectively preclude the possibility of any single state pursuing an independent economic policy.

Authoritarianism
A complementary authoritarian thrust likewise remains visible across Western Europe, differentiated only by the degree and manner of its formulation. The 1980s have seen a steady increase in government powers in Britain and Belgium, coupled with the

legal contraction of trade-union and other rights. The retraction of trade-union rights has also gone ahead in Greece and West Germany. This indicates that contrary to the protestations of politicians who claim to be 'rolling back the State', there has been a sharp and widespread concentration of power over the last decade in the hands of central governments, technocracies and big business.

Where democratic reforms have been conceded, as for example in the extension of education and of women's rights in Spain, they have been carried out primarily as social adjuncts to the process of economic modernisation. Meanwhile racism, fostered by 'respectable' political parties, has continued to spread. Although Le Pen's *Front National* was eclipsed at the parliamentary level in 1988, there is continued evidence of extensive racist sentiment in France and growing support for similarly inclined parties in Denmark and Norway in 1987.[3]

But if in some states New Conservative policies have become unpopular, the coordinates of the conservative project none the less remain. The combination of economic liberalism with varying degrees of social and political authoritarianism looks set to define the parameters of West European politics into the 1990s. Over the large part of the region the lineaments of the New Conservatism have come to replace both older forms of quasi-fascist conservatism and the social democracy of the post-war period.

In acknowledging this shift, it is important to be clear about the kind of societies that the New Conservative politics is currently shaping.

The Social Consequences

'Brazilianisation'

The first and most profound effect is to precipitate the process graphically described by Goran Therborn as 'Brazilianisation': the formation of a large, permanent, underemployed and welfare-dependent 'residuum' at one end of the spectrum, and an increasing concentration of wealth at the other, with the bulk of the employed situated more or less precariously in between.[4] The persistence of high levels of unemployment is one index of this development. By the end of 1987, despite alleged economic recovery over the previous four years, the official rate of unemployment was still over 10 per cent in France, Belgium, Greece, the Netherlands, Italy, and Britain, while in Spain it was over 20 per cent.

Another symptom is the accelerating inequality in the distribution of wealth and the expansion of the pool of poverty. Thatcher's Britain has become something of a prototype in this regard, as statistics grimly reveal. Thus the average tax cut (about $41,000) conceded to the richest 210,000 taxpayers in the 1988 budget was greater than the *income* of any taxpayer in the bottom 95 per cent of the income scale. Concomitantly, 'the value of the pay of the poorest ten per cent of workers relative to the national average is now at an all-time record low – lower than when the figures were first collected in 1888.'[5]

Moreover, the number of people whose incomes were below the accepted 'poverty line' doubled to 12 million between 1979 and 1987, one-fifth of the entire population.[6] Little wonder, therefore, that a French journalist visiting the capital of the 'enterprise culture' could reach a caustic conclusion: 'apparemment, Londres se tiers-mondise.'[7]

The New Underclass

This emerging social formation has numerous implications, the most serious of which is the marginalisation of a substantial section of the working class from the mainstream of economic, social and political life. Participating – if at all – only in the 'hidden' or 'black' economy, such groups, among whom women, youth and the ethnic minorities are disproportionately represented, form a cheap casual labour force operating outside the channels of legal employment and union organisation.

The decentralisation of production and the growth of a low-wage service sector, as well as the 'deregulation' measures of governments in the field of employment, have produced a rapid growth in these marginal areas of economic activity. Reliable statistics are hard to come by, but the 'black' economy is estimated to employ as many as 3.5 million workers in Italy and to account for 20-25 per cent of Gross Domestic Product (GDP) in Portugal.[8]

Beyond the stylised images of the 'enterprise culture', in other words, lie the permanently unemployed and a swelling, unofficial and low-paid workforce that are its inevitable corollary. It is towards this expanded 'underclass', constituted as a social problem, that the welfare state is increasingly directed. Governments now seek to reduce levels of taxation and state expenditure by encouraging the majority of the employed population to look to the private sector for health care, education, retirement pensions and so on. Welfare provision is deliberately reduced to release cash for redistribution to private enterprise in the form of tax cuts and investment incentives. Squeezing welfare benefits simultaneously serves to lower wages, by forcing the unemployed to accept work at reduced rates of pay.

It is not a subtle strategy, but it is tried and tested, as any acquaintance with the utilitarian underpinnings of Victorian social policy will illustrate.

The Electoral Strategy

The New Conservative conception of society thus envisages two nations under one State, divided by their access to the labour and consumer markets. As a political strategy it is feasible primarily because the 'ins' outnumber the 'outs' – hence Peter Glotz's description of this as the 'two-thirds/one-third society'.[9] For one of the features of the last decade is that despite economic recession and high levels of unemployment, the real incomes of the majority of those *in full-time work* have continued to rise. This has been the case not only in the most affluent states, such as West Germany, but also where poverty has increased most dramatically, like Britain.

In almost all West European countries there is an inbuilt majority – the 'two-thirds' – which has materially benefited from New Conservative policies, or can hope to. Yet it is noteworthy that such policies have, on the whole, not needed an electoral majority to be implemented: in West Germany, France and Britain right-wing governments were comfortably elected in the 1980s with less than half the vote, thanks in each case to the divided nature of the opposition. But in either event the result in electoral terms is that the economically marginal one-third is rendered politically marginal, a voiceless presence in society.

Contracting the Debate

The process of Brazilianisation inevitably hits hardest those who in the short term are least able to fight back, the new 'underclass' who lack both economic and political representation. But it also has wider repercussions for the political culture as a whole. It narrows the parameters of political debate by limiting the terms on which particular subjects are publicly discussed, or by excluding certain themes altogether.

Mass unemployment, for example, has been gradually erased from the political agenda during the course of the 1980s. As early as 1983 *The Times* in Britain could greet the Conservatives' election victory as evidence that 'the tired attempt to invest the phenomenon of unemployment with some statistical morality has not taken in the electors.'[10] Five years later, with unemployment still running over 10 per cent, the French presidential election was conducted almost entirely without reference to the issue.

Similarly, the conservative emphasis on notions of 'enterprise' and 'cost-effectiveness' ensures that the voter is appealed to in the exclusive guise of 'economic man' (sic): tax-payer, rate-payer, property-owner, consumer. The idea of 'value-for-money' comes to replace any broader conception of 'social need' or the 'public good'. What is reflected here is a recognition that political discourse need refer only to the comfortable 'two-thirds', the residual one-third lying for the most part outside these categories.

Not only does this shift reflect astounding political cynicism, it also has implications for our political culture as a whole. What is suppressed is a range of social identities that cannot be subsumed within the new class grouping: individuals, with social rights as well as economic interests, citizens, as well as property-owners, women, as well as men, with specific social needs. The notion of 'economic man' that has come to stand as the yardstick of conservative discourse offers a woefully inadequate reflection of the proliferation of people's social identities, and the demands they have, in contemporary European societies.

Limiting Democracy

The unavoidable corollary of this foreclosing of economic and political access to the State by the members of a society, is a starkly reduced conception of democracy. The 1980s have seen the steady transfer of residual powers from popular hands to dominant political elites. This trend has been apparent on the left as well as the right. The socialist parties in southern Europe, like PASOK and the PSOE, that came to power in the late 1970s and early 1980s on the back of mass mobilisation and support, have been particularly conspicuous in their subsequent concentration of power in the hands of their own leadership and directive bureaucracies.

Not only have local government, the trade unions, grass-roots party organisations – some of the institutional channels for democratic participation – been severely restricted, the State itself has become ever more secretive, as the Zircon affair in Britain and the 'Rainbow Warrior' case in France testify.

There are also more direct political repercussions. The system of parliamentary democracy installed in most Western European states after 1945 was based on the idea that government would be shared between alternating parties. But as parties espousing versions of the New Conservatism have consolidated their hold on government in the 1980s, so countries like Britain, Greece, Spain, Portugal and Italy have come increasingly to resemble one-party states with clientilist governments manipulating the levers of power and patronage to monopolise public office. The 'Brazilianisation' of social formations is accompanied by the 'Mexicanisation' of political systems.[11]

By any standards these are dangerous tendencies, damaging not only to those who bear the brunt of poverty, unemployment and sexual or racial harassment, but to the very conception of a democratic political culture. Any politics that envisages consigning a substantial section of the population to social, economic and political limbo cannot properly be called democratic. It resembles, rather, a form of unofficial apartheid, in which the 'other nation' is stripped of its tenuous claims to acceptance as partners within a notional social contract, and is reconstituted outside the contractual bounds as a moral and law-and-order problem. As Ralf Dahrendorf puts it,

> the existence of an underclass casts doubt on the social contract itself. It means that citizenship has become an exclusive rather than an inclusive status. Some are full citizens, some are not.[12]

Yet this is precisely the order of society that the New Conservatism is working to shape.

The Consequences for Socialism

I have tried in this study to indicate something of the nature and dimensions of the New Conservatism in Western Europe, not to suggest simple answers to it, still less a blueprint for its supercession by a revitalised socialism. But there are equally clearly a number of conclusions that inescapably impose themselves on the future prospects of the European left.

The first and most obvious verdict is that almost everywhere the West European left badly underestimated the depth of the crisis that developed from the 1970s, and the capacity of conservatism to capitalise upon it. This was evident in states like Britain, West Germany, Belgium and the Netherlands, where the right was able to benefit from the disarray of the labour movement and governing socialist parties, and to diagnose variable doses of economic neo-liberalism as the sole cure for economic ills.

In many cases, the left was especially vulnerable because it had paved the way for such prescriptions in government, and because the labour movement as a whole had no viable alternative that did not envisage the maintenance of an increasingly barren status quo. The extent to which the parliamentary and trade-union left had become embroiled in the crisis in Britain and West Germany partly explains the painful slowness of its response to it. It was not until the mid-1980s that the left began to register the radical nature of the New Conservative politics.

Indeed, it is still questionable whether the major changes wrought in the political landscape over the last decade have yet been fully absorbed by the major political parties. Significant elements on the centre or right of the SPD, the PCI and the British Labour Party *still* appear to believe that a return to the social democratic consensus of the 1960s and early 1970s is feasible. Even were this desirable, which is doubtful, it is now no more than a political pipe-dream. Not only are the necessary economic and social conditions provided by the 'long boom' and powerful supportive trade-union movements no longer in place, the ideological consensus that justified interventionist management of the economy in the name of 'social justice' has been effectively ruptured.

But such a belief also overlooks the experience of socialist governments in Western Europe during the 1980s, their acceptance of the logic of neo-liberal economics, and their retreat into greater or lesser degrees of social conservatism and political authoritarianism.

There is, in practice, no longer any any viable model of socialism in Western Europe. The southern parties of the left either have no prospect of power in the foreseeable future (like the PCI), or else cannot be considered socialist in any meaningful sense (like the PSOE). Nor can Sweden, for so long the paragon of a practicable welfare socialism and still considered as such in many quarters, be taken as a feasible alternative. In the first place, Swedish social democracy is the product of the particular conjunction of an unprecedentedly powerful labour movement and a political party, the SDP, which has enjoyed the longest historical record of office of any Western party. Such conditions are not repeatable elsewhere. Secondly, as this study has shown, Swedish social democracy has itself been thrown onto the defensive in the 1980s. It can no longer be regarded as the radical force it briefly appeared during the Wage-Earner Funds debate in the 1970s.

Rethinking on the Left

Economic Alternatives

It is clear, therefore, that socialism will have to be rebuilt politically as well as electorally – indeed the former is a precondition of the latter. Rethinking is required on a whole number of fronts. Of most immediate importance is the elaboration of an economic alternative to the neo-liberal 'open economy' model currently favoured, not only by large capital and the right, but also by existing socialist governments.

There are some signs that labour movements in northern Europe in particular are beginning to reconsider basic assumptions concerning the relation between public and private ownership, and the directive role of the State in economic management. But it is by no means clear whether this represents a simple concession to the priorities of the right, with a milder, more 'socially-conscious' version of market economics, or an attempt to lay the groundwork for a new 'post-statist' approach to socialist economic policy.

On the whole, it would appear that the parties in Britain and West Germany at least are veering more towards the former. The Labour Party's review in 1988 argued that the State should only intervene where the market is obviously deficient, as in research and development. It rejected proposals to reverse Conservative tax-cuts to the higher-paid.[13] Similarly, according to observers, the SPD's new programme was 'likely to contain a *more* positive appraisal of the market economy than its predecessor'.[14]

At present, much of the European left appears to be caught on the horns of a dilemma: either follow the well-trodden path towards the Scylla of the 'open economy'; or revert to the Charybdis of central planning and state ownership. In fact, neither option is likely to prove fruitful. The known and disastrous effects on the working class of unfettered economic individualism should preclude the former path. It is an index of the vitiated state of socialist ideology that parties in the 1980s should end by defending the very model of free-market capitalism, opposition to which was the primary reason for their original existence.

Nor is the extension of state ownership through a full programme of nationalisation any longer a viable course. The corporate manner in which nationalisation was carried out in the majority of post-war European states signally failed to redistribute power to the working class. Furthermore, given the increasingly complex multinational character of capital, its tendency to operate diffusely through sub-contracting, franchising and an international division of labour, it is no longer practicable for any individual State to undertake such a programme.

Alternative approaches to the 'open economy' model have been developed by socialist organisations at the local level in Italy, Britain and elsewhere during the 1980s. These have tended to emphasise the importance of the social control of industries and enterprises, rather than their ownership by the State. The idea of a 'public economy' is retained, but the directive agency would be provided by a variety of municipal, cooperative and voluntary bodies, not by the central State alone.[15] As yet, the influence of such approaches is only dimly apparent in the economic programmes of labour parties at national level, although they have found a more receptive audience in the trade-union movement. Yet the commitment of parties of the left to some form of public economy is clearly necessary, not only as an antidote to 'popular capitalism', but also to avoid the trap of merely posing as more efficient managers of the capitalist economy.

The State and Citizenship

Equally innovative approaches will need to be elaborated in relation to the State as a whole. The identification of socialist parties with bureaucratic centralism has been a potent source of their unpopularity, and one which the 'anti-statism' of right-wing interests has exploited to considerable effect. Less thought has been given to the future of the State than to economic questions, but it is likely to be no less important to the revival of the left. It will be essential, for example, to go beyond a simple defence of the welfare state, to concrete proposals on how health or welfare provision can be improved and made responsive to those who use their services.[16]

Such rethinking requires a deeper commitment to the emancipatory goals of socialism than the traditional institutions of the left seem yet prepared to envisage. To construct the model of an 'enabling State' demands more than mere constitutional rights – freedom of information or electoral reform – however desirable these are. It demands, in the first place, a whole new set of institutional arrangements designed to link the State to civil society and to allow for greater popular participation in decision-making.[17] Despite the appeals for extending democracy, no socialist or labour party in Western Europe has yet proposed an institutional reform that would significantly expand the possibility of popular participation. Parties of the left have proved scarcely less mistrusting of the self-activation of the working class than their conservative counterparts. But without such a concept of popular democracy, the left remains vulnerable to the notion of 'freedom of choice' based on spending-power, which passes, on the right, for an extension of democracy.

A reformed State requires, secondly, a concept of social citizenship that goes beyond the minimum right to material sufficiency, towards a positive recognition of the diversity of social needs. The 'new politics' has uncovered the range of concerns, from the environment to sexuality, that shape the political perceptions of growing numbers of people. Yet these perceptions find little reflection in the politics of both left and right, which both remain obsessed in different ways with the figure of 'economic man'. From the standpoint of the left, what this emphasises is that the new politics of feminism, of race and ecology will have to be integrated with the politics of labour in more fundamental ways than have yet been considered necessary. It demands a politics fully recommitted to the goals of social, as well as economic, emancipation.

Internationalism

In short, if parties and movements of the left are to regain momentum, they will need to be as radical in their thrust and aims as the New Conservatism has proved to be. They will also need to be more internationalist in outlook and practice than hitherto. For, as Goran Therborn notes, 'there is, in fact, distressingly little communication between socialists of different countries compared with the constant, smooth dialogue between and within multinational corporations.'[18] The coordination of socialist movements has become all the more pressing as capital is internationalised, and 1992, when European neo-liberalism receives its official imprimatur, approaches.

Such international linkage is not without precedent in the 1980s. The dialogue and cooperation between, for example, national peace movements in Eastern and Western Europe is indicative of the ways in which parties and movements can link up, with impressive political results. But an extension of such linkages in Western Europe and abroad – between trade unions organising to counter the operations of multinationals, between public economies for the exchange of goods, services and information, and between governments for the coordination of economic policy – must prove indispensable to the creation of a sustainable socialist order. Because 'for all practical purposes', as one commentator recently stated, 'Keynesianism in one country is now as utopian a notion as socialism in one country.'[19]

The Historic Moment

The political situation in Western Europe today could be said to resemble that in the 1850s, when the radical mass movements in France, Britain, the Low Countries and the Austro-Hungarian Empire stood uniformly defeated by the combined forces of political reaction and economic liberalism. But within two decades a new mass labour movement was forming, headed in many cases by socialist parties, and united in opposition to capitalism. The same period also saw the birth of an organised feminist movement. In the years before, during and immediately after the First World War, these forces were able to mount a challenge to the dominant order in Europe. Their challenge permanently transformed the social and political landscape.

The task confronting the left in the late 1980s is scarcely less daunting. Yet as the struggle to create a new politics, to recover a sense of the future, begins, it is worth recalling what history repeatedly demonstrates. Victory may be ephemeral, but defeat is never permanent.

Notes

Introduction: New Wine in Old Bottles

1. G. Marks, 'The Revival of *Laisser-faire*', in R. Hodder-Williams and J. Caesar, eds, *Politics in Britain and the United States* (Durham: Duke University Press, 1986) pp. 28–54.
2. H. Rogger and E. Weber, eds, *The European Right: A Historical Profile* (Berkeley: University of California Press, 1966); N. O'Sullivan, *Conservatism* (London: Dent, 1976) Chapter 1.
3. For a discussion of German development and the origins of fascism, see D. Blackbourn and G. Eley, *The Peculiarities of German History: Bourgeois Society and Politics in Nineteenth Century Germany* (Oxford: Oxford University Press, 1984). For the continuities in Spanish fascism, see R. Fraser, *Blood Of Spain. The Experience of Civil War, 1936–1939* (Harmondsworth: Penguin, 1981) Chapter 1.
4. N. Harris, *Competition and the Corporate State: British Conservatives, the State and Industry, 1945–1964* (London: Methuen, 1972).
5. The first race riots in Britain occurred in Notting Hill Gate, London in 1958. Poujadism was a political movement of small business and peasant farmers in mid-1950s France. It combined protest against taxation and state bureaucracy with a strong dose of anti-semitic sentiment. The movement was named after its leader, Pierre Poujade; it gained 2.5 million votes and 52 seats at the 1956 elections.
6. 'Conservative Politics, Work, Socialism and Utopia Today: Interview with Hans-Ulrich Rech, 2 April 1983', in P. Dews, ed, *Habermas: Autonomy and Solidarity* (London: Verso, 1986) pp. 136–7.

Chapter 1: The Retreat from Social Democracy

1. Thatcher's statement was widely commented on in the run-up to the 1987 general election. See S. Hall, 'Blue Election, Election Blues', *Marxism Today*, July 1987, for a discussion of the ideological issues at stake.
2. *Nouvel Observateur*, 5 June 1987.
3. *The Liberal Imagination* (London: Secker and Warburg, 1951).
4. A. Werth, *France 1940–1955* (London: Robert Hale, 1957) Chapter 13;

S.J. Woolf, ed, *The Rebirth of Italy, 1943–50* (London: Longman, 1972).

5. For a summary see M.E. Streit, 'Germany: Economic Developments, Problems and Policies', in J.P. Payne, ed, *Germany Today* (London: Methuen, 1971).

6. A. Sked and C. Cook, *Post-War Britain: A Political History* (Harmondsworth: Penguin, 1986) pp. 50, 84.

7. T. Prittie, *Konrad Adenauer 1876–1967* (London: Tom Stacey, 1972) pp. 217–18 and 230–1.

8. D. Acheson, *Present at the Creation* (New York: Norton, 1969) p. 217.

9. E. Hobsbawm, *Industry and Empire* (Harmondsworth: Penguin, 1979) p. 247.

10. For comments see P. Anderson, 'The Figures of Descent', *New Left Review* No. 161, Jan–Feb 1987, pp. 73–4.

11. *Politics and Society* Vol. 11, No. 4, p. 402.

12. *Political Man* (London: Heinemann, 1960) p. 406.

13. C. Leys, *Politics in Britain* (London: Verso, 1986) Chapter 6.

14. Leys, *Politics*, p. 119.

15. For a discussion see Claudia von Braunmühl, 'The Attack on Civil Rights in West Germany', *Radical Philosophy* No. 19, Spring 1978.

16. H. Wachtel, *The Politics of International Money* (Amsterdam: Transnational Institute, 1987) p. 35.

17. R. Murray, 'Ownership, Control and the Market', *New Left Review* No. 164, Jul–Aug 1987, p. 91.

18. 'The Post-Reagan Economy: a New Democratic Deal', *World Policy Journal*, Spring 1986, p. 186.

19. *The End of the Third World* (London: Penguin 1987) pp. 201-2.

20. *Why Some People are More Unemployed than Others* (London: Verso, 1986) p. 23.

21. *Life Chances: Approaches to Social and Political Theory* (London: Weidenfeld and Nicolson, 1979) pp. 106–7.

Chapter 2: The Politics and Ideology of Conservatism in the 1980s

1. A. Gamble, 'The Political Economy of Freedom', in R. Levitas, ed, *The Ideology of the New Right* (Cambridge: Polity Press, 1986).

2. D. Graham and P. Clarke, *The New Enlightenment* (London: Macmillan, 1986) pp. 16–18. See also C.J. Friedrich, 'The Political Thought of Neo-Liberalism', *American Political Science Review*, Vol. XLIX, 1955, pp. 509–25.

3. G.H. Nash, *The Conservative Intellectual Movement in America since 1945* (New York: Basic Books, 1976) p. 26.

4. R. Nozick, *Anarchy, State and Utopia* (Oxford: Blackwell, 1974).

5. 'The Heritage Foundation Goes Abroad', in *The Nation*, 6 June 1987.
6. For an historical overview see Eugen Weber, 'France', in Rogger and Weber, *European Right*.
7. 'L'extrème-droite en France: enquête', in *Nouvel Observateur*, June 1987.
8. A. Bell, 'Against Racism and Fascism in Europe', pamphlet of the Socialist Group in the European Parliament, 1986, p. 15.
9. 'Far Right in Scandinavia', *Economist*, 28 May 1988.
10. M. Vaughan, 'Nouvelle droite: Cultural Power and Political Influence', in D.S. Bell, ed, *Contemporary French Political Parties* (London: Croom Helm, 1982) pp. 52ff.
11. F. Gress, 'The New Right in France and the Federal Republic of Germany', in N. Deakin, ed, *The New Right: Image and Reality* (London: Runnymede Trust, 1986) p. 53.
12. B. Rowthorn and J. Wells, *Deindustrialisation and Foreign Trade* (Cambridge: Cambridge University Press, 1987).
13. 'Primitive privatisations', *Economist*, 29 June 1986.
14. Privatisation survey, *Financial Times*, 16 Sept 1987, p. 2.
15. E. Balladur, *Nouvel Observateur*, 12 Sept 1986.
16. *Nouvel Observateur*, 5 June 1987.
17. Privatisation survey, *Financial Times*, 16 Sept 1987, p. 2
18. Privatisation survey, *Financial Times*, 16 Sept 1987, p. 2.
19. West Germany survey, *Economist*, 6 Dec 1986.
20. Privatisation survey, *Financial Times*, 16 Sept 1987, p. 7.
21. *Economist*, 11 Apr 1987, p. 13.
22. *Economist*, 10 Oct 1987, p. 91.
23. J. Palmer, 'Sweeping Away the Barriers', *Guardian*, 9 Oct 1987.
24. For a recent discussion see J. Hayward, *The State and the Market Economy: Industrial Patriotism and Economic Intervention in France* (Brighton: Wheatsheaf Books, 1986).
25. M. Wiener, *English Culture and the Decline of the Industrial Spirit* (Cambridge: Cambridge University Press, 1982) p. 8.
26. R. Harris, 'Prima Donna Inter Pares', *Observer*, 3 Jan 1988.
27. 'Revolt of the Spirit', *New Socialist*, Feb 1987, pp. 9–11.
28. *Nouvel Observateur*, 12 Sept 1986, p. 11.
29. *Social Trends* (London: HMSO, 1980 and 1987).
30. E. Balladur, *Nouvel Observateur*, 5 June 1987.
31. P. Walters, 'The Legacy of Olof Palme: the Condition of the Swedish Model', *Government and Opposition*, Winter 1987, pp. 72ff.
32. 'Storming the Town Halls', *Marxism Today*, Apr 1984, pp. 8–9.
33. *Economist*, 22 Feb 1986.
34. 'La nouvelle droite et ses stratégies', *Nouvelle Revue Socialiste*, May 1984.

35. *Independent*, 25 Apr 1988, p. 11.
36. *Observer*, 24 May 1987.
37. *Independent*, 25 Apr 1988, p. 11.
38. *Guardian*, 24 Sept 1987.
39. Bell, 'Against Racism', p. 8.
40. G. Seidel, 'Culture, Nation and "Race"', in Levitas, ed, *Ideology*, p. 114.
41. Ibid.
42. G. Smith, 'Consequences of the West German Election', in *Government and Opposition*, Spring 1987, pp. 131ff.
43. S. Hall et al., *Policing the Crisis: Mugging, the State and Law and Order* (London: Macmillan, 1978).
44. See for example F. Palmer, ed, *Anti-Racism: An Assault on Education and Values* (Nottingham: Sherwood Press, 1987).
45. C. Hall and L. Davidoff, 'Home, Sweet Home', *New Statesman*, 27 May 1983.
46. Graham and Clarke, *New Enlightenment*, p. 67.
47. G. Gilder, *Wealth and Poverty* (New York: Basic Books, 1982).
48. For a discussion see B. Fitzpatrick, 'The Sex Discrimination Act 1986', in *Modern Law Review*, Vol. 50, No. 7, Nov 1987, pp. 934–51.
49. B. Ehrenreich, *The Hearts of Men: American Dreams and the Flight from Commitment* (New York: Doubleday, 1983) p. 172.
50. P. Townsend, *Why are the Many Poor?* (London: Fabian Tracts, 1984) p. 17.
51. J. Watts, 'The Power Game', *Observer*, 24 Apr 1988, p. 33.
52. J. Weeks, *Sex, Politics and Society* (London: Longman, 1981) p. 274.
53. *Marxism Today*, Aug 1987.
54. Dews, *Habermas*, pp. 82ff.
55. C. Ysmal, 'Forces et faiblesses de la doctrine du national-populisme', in Alain Mayer, ed, *Le Libéralisme dans le monde* (Paris: *Nouvelle Revue Socialiste*, 1986) p. 100.
56. S. Hall, 'Thatcher's Lessons', *Marxism Today*, Mar 1988.
57. The origins of Margaret Thatcher's political philosophy are discussed in D. Kavanagh, *Thatcherism and British Politics: The End of Consensus?* (Oxford: Oxford University Press, 1986).
58. D. Sassoon, 'Italy's Fading Dream', in *Marxism Today*, Aug 1987.

Chapter 3: The Constituencies and Appeal of Conservatism

1. See for example R. Inglehart, *The Silent Revolution: Changing Values and Political Styles Among Western Publics* (Princeton: Princeton University Press, 1977).

2. As they have consistently in the past, see Rogger and Weber, 'European Right'.

3. *Sunday Times*, 14 June 1987; S. Padgett and T. Burkett, *Political Parties and Elections in West Germany* (London: Hurst, 1986) p. 265.

4. Padgett and Burkett, *Political Parties*, p. 265.

5. F. Bechofer and B. Elliott, eds, *Petite Bourgeoisie: Comparative Studies of the Uneasy Stratum* (London: Macmillan, 1983).

6. D.P. Conradt and R.J. Dalton, 'The West German Electorate and the Party System: Continuity and Change in the 1980s', *Review of Politics*, Winter 1988, pp. 3–29.

7. *Sunday Times*, 14 June 1987.

8. P.A. Daniels, 'The End of the Craxi Era? The Italian Parliamentary Elections of 1987', *Parliamentary Affairs*, Apr 1988, pp. 258–86.

9. D. Corkill, 'The Portuguese Election of 1987', *Parliamentary Affairs*, Apr 1988, pp. 247–57.

10. E. Hobsbawm, 'Out of the Wilderness', *Marxism Today*, Oct 1987, p. 12.

11. *Guardian*, 15 June 1987 and 2 Nov 1988, p. 25.

12. See Chapter 4 for a fuller discussion.

13. Leys, *Politics*, p. 89; *Sunday Times*, 14 June 1987.

14. Padgett and Burkett, *Political Parties*, p. 265.

15. Sassoon, 'Italy's Fading Dream'.

16. For Austria see M.A. Sully, 'Austrian Social Democracy', in W.E. Paterson and A.H. Thomas, eds, *The Future of Social Democracy: Problems and Prospects of Social Democratic Parties in Western Europe* (Oxford: Clarendon Press, 1986).

17. See D. Massey, 'Heartlands of Defeat', *Marxism Today*, July 1987. A similar pattern is evident elsewhere, in Belgium, the Netherlands and West Germany. For example, despite the drift of skilled workers to the right, the German SPD increased its vote in 1987 in Saarland, Lower Saxony and North-Rhine Westphalia. All these states belong to the so-called 'rust-belt' of declining industries. For details see R. Irving and W.E. Paterson, 'The West German Election of 1987', in *Parliamentary Affairs*, Vol. 40, No. 3, July 1987, p. 351ff.

18. Though the issue is complex and contested. See for example I. Crewe and D. Denver, eds, *Electoral Change in Western Democracies* (London: Croom Helm, 1985).

19. *Libération*, 18 Mar 1986.

20. *Independent*, 29 Apr 1988. A sociological profile shows that in the 1988 presidential election, Le Pen attracted 31% of the votes of artisans and small shopkeepers, 16% of junior management, 11% of office and shopworkers, 18% of small farmers, 21% of professionals, 16% of the working-class vote and 19% of the unemployed; G. Jenkins, 'The

Threat of Le Pen', *Socialist Worker Review*, June 1988.

21. Down 11% on the equivalent 1983 figure for women in the 18–24 age group, 5% in the 25–34 group and 3% overall. *Sunday Times*, 14 June 1987.
22. Padgett and Burkett, *Political Parties*, p. 282.
23. Daniels, 'End of the Craxi Era'.
24. Corkill, 'Portuguese Election'.
25. *Guardian*, 30 Apr 1988.
26. C. Ysmal, 'Les français et le libéralisme', in Alain Mayer, ed, *Le Libéralisme dans le monde*.
27. J. Krieger, *Reagan, Thatcher and the Politics of Decline* (Cambridge: Polity Press, 1986) p. 87; G. Heald and R.J. Wybrow, *The Gallup Survey of Britain* (London: Croom Helm, 1986) p. 144.
28. Padgett and Burkett, *Political Parties*, p. 243; Paterson and Thomas, *Future of Social Democracy*, p. 41.
29. Hobsbawm, *Industry and Empire*, p. 248.
30. Ysmal, 'Libéralisme', p. 127.
31. Heald and Wybrow, *Gallup*, pp. 96–101.
32. Ibid.
33. D. Webber, 'Social Democracy and the Re-emergence of Mass Unemployment in Western Europe', in Paterson and Thomas, *Future of Social Democracy*, p. 57.
34. *Forschungsgruppe Wahlen* (Mannheim) June 1980, Feb 1983 and Jan 1987 surveys.
35. L. Morlino, 'The Changing Relationship between Parties and Society in Italy', in S. Bartolini and P. Mair, eds, *Party Politics In Contemporary Western Europe* (London: Cass, 1984) pp. 56–63.
36. P. Norton, 'Britain: Still a Two-party System?' in Bartolini and Mair, *Party Politics*, pp. 33–5.
37. *Observer*, 25 Jan 1987.
38. *Europe as Seen by Europeans: European Polling 1973–1986* (Brussels: EC, 1986) pp. 62–3.
39. Krieger, *Reagan, Thatcher*, p. 77.
40. *Nouvel Observateur*, 5 June 1987.
41. Ysmal, 'Libéralisme', p. 129.
42. Ibid., p. 127.
43. Kavanagh, *Thatcherism*, p. 296.
44. Ibid., p. 293.
45. Ysmal, 'Libéralisme', p. 127.
46. E. Hobsbawm, 'Ostpolitik Reborn', *Marxism Today*, Aug 1987.
47. Portugal survey, *Economist*, 28 May 1988.
48. BBC Gallup survey, June 1983.
49. G.H. Gallup, *The International Gallup Polls* (London: Greenwood

Press, 1980) p. 141.
50. Heald and Wybrow, *Gallup*, p. 185.
51. Her rating as a 'strong personality' rose from 84% to 95% between 1977 and 1985; but the proportion that saw her as 'dividing the country' rose from 31% to 71% over the same period. Heald and Wybrow, *Gallup*, pp. 29–30.
52. The Westland affair erupted when the Defence Minister, Michael Heseltine, openly opposed the Thatcher government's decision to allow the Westland helicopter company to be sold to an American firm, rather than accept a European rescue bid. In the process, not only were Heseltine and another minister, Leon Brittan, forced to resign, but the Prime Minister was widely held to have lied to Parliament and to have behaved in a dictatorial manner within the Cabinet.
53. Ysmal, 'Libéralisme', pp. 128–9.
54. Heald and Wybrow, *Gallup*, pp. 127, 131.
55. Ysmal, 'Libéralisme', p. 129.
56. Heald and Wybrow, *Gallup*, p. 112.
57. Ysmal, 'Libéralisme', p. 129.
58. D. Sassoon, *Contemporary Italy: Politics, Economy and Society Since 1945* (London: Longman, 1986) pp. 108–9, 224.
59. Heald and Wybrow, *Gallup*, p. 91.

Chapter 4: Playing the Game: The Role of the Left in Europe

1. See for example A. Gorz, *Farewell to the Working Class: An Essay on Post-Industrial Socialism* (London: Pluto Press, 1982); A. Touraine, *Post-Industrial Society: Tomorrow's Social History* (London: Wildwood House, 1974); E. Hobsbawm, *The Forward March of Labour Halted* (London: New Left Books, 1981).
2. G. Therborn, 'Britain Left Out', in J. Curran, ed, *The Future of the Left* (Cambridge: Polity Press, 1984) pp. 125–37.
3. Sassoon, 'Italy's Fading Dream'.
4. N. Ascherson, 'The Man who was a Monument', *Observer*, 29 Mar 1987.
5. For an historical overview see J. Hinton, *Labour and Socialism: A History of the British Labour Movement 1867–1974* (Brighton: Wheatsheaf Books, 1983).
6. V. Bognador and R. Skidelsky, *The Age of Affluence* (London: Macmillan, 1970) p. 10.
7. *Labour's Programme 1983* (London: Labour Party, 1983).
8. Leys, *Politics*, Chapter 5.

9. Cited in W.E. Paterson and D. Webber, 'The Federal Republic of Germany: the Re-emergent Opposition?' in E. Kolinsky, ed, *Opposition in Western Europe* (London: Croom Helm, 1987) p. 136.
10. See von Braunmühl, 'Attack on Civil Rights'.
11. Cited by Paterson and Webber, 'Federal Republic'.
12. Padgett and Burkett, *Political Parties*, p. 61.
13. G. Braunthal, *The West German Social Democrats, 1969–82* (Boulder: Westview, 1983) pp. 88–97.
14. See D. Sassoon, *The Strategy of the Italian Communist Party: From the Resistance to the Historic Compromise* (London: Frances Pinter, 1981).
15. G. Aymot, *The Italian Communist Party: The Crisis of the Popular Front Strategy* (London: Croom Helm, 1981) Chapter 11.
16. Sassoon, *Contemporary Italy*, p. 237.
17. '*Il Manifesto* and Italian Communism: an Interview with Luciana Castellina', in *New Left Review* No. 151, May–June 1985, p. 33.
18. For a discussion see J.S. Ambler, ed, *The French Socialist Experiment* (Philadelphia: ISHI, 1985).
19. 'What Mitterrand and His Men Have Actually Done', *Economist*, 8 Mar 1986, p. 50.
20. 'Co-existentialism in France', *The Nation*, 17 May 1986, p. 694.
21. B. Criddle, 'France: Legitimacy Attained', in Kolinsky, ed, *Opposition in Western Europe*, p. 120.
22. Cited in P. Lane, *Europe Since 1945* (London: Batsford, 1985) p. 184.
23. P. Camiller, 'Spanish Socialism in the Atlantic Order', *New Left Review* No. 156, Mar–Apr 1986, pp. 5ff.
24. M. Threlfall, 'The Women's Movement in Spain', *New Left Review* No. 151, May–June 1985, p. 64.
25. Camiller, 'Spanish Socialism'.
26. P. Heywood, 'Spain: 10 June 1987', in *Government and Opposition*, Autumn 1987, pp. 390–401.
27. 'Choppy Waters in the Med', *Economist*, 11 Apr 1987, p. 54.
28. 'The Rise and Decline of the Southern European Socialist Parties', *New Left Review* No. 146, July–Aug 1984, pp. 37ff.
29. M. Rhodes and V. Wright, 'The European Steel Unions and the Steel Crisis, 1974–84', *British Journal of Political Science*, Apr 1988, pp. 171ff.
30. HMSO, *Social Trends*; Heywood, 'Spain'.
31. J. Pontusson, 'Radicalisation and Retreat in Swedish Social Democracy', *New Left Review* No. 165, Sept–Oct 1987, pp. 5–33.
32 Rhodes and Wright, 'European Steel Unions'.
33. J. Lloyd, 'Parting of the Ways', *Marxism Today*, Apr 1988.
34. D. Johnstone, 'How the French learned to Love the Bomb', *New Left*

Review No. 146, July–Aug 1984.

35. F. Bianchini, 'Living for the City', *New Socialist*, Apr 1987, p. 15.
36. Threlfall, 'Women's Movement', p. 46.
37. *Marxism Today*, Aug 1987.
38. *Towards 2000* (London: Hogarth Press, 1983) p. 253.
39. 'The Transformation of Extra-parliamentary Opposition in West Germany, and the Peace Movement', in Kolinsky, ed, *Opposition in Western Europe*, p. 315.
40. Morrissey, *The Smiths in Quotes* (Todmorden: Babylon, 1985) p. 17.

Conclusion: The Shape of Politics to Come

1. 'An Arch with Two Pillars', interview with Peter Jenkins, *Independent*, 23 May 1988.
2. J. Robinson, 'The EC Commission: A New-found Friend of Business', *Europe*, Nov 1986, pp. 18–20.
3. See Chapter 2 for details.
4. Therborn, *Why Some People are More Unemployed than Others*, pp. 32ff.
5. F. Field, *Guardian*, 1 Aug 1988.
6. Figures in J. Rentoul, *The Rich Get Richer* (London: Unwin, 1987).
7. 'La botte de Thatcher', *Nouvel Observateur*, 5 June 1987.
8. Portugal survey, *Economist*, 28 May 1988; Sassoon, *Contemporary Italy*, p. 75.
9. 'Forward to Europe', *Dissent*, Summer 1986.
10. 11 June 1983.
11. The term 'Mexicanisation' is used to denote permanent one-party rule in a parliamentary democracy, achieved by patronage and manipulation. It derives from Mexico, where the *Partido Revolucionario Institucional* (PRI) has managed to control the presidency, the congress and the state governments since the 1920s.
12. *New Statesman*, 12 June 1987.
13. *Independent*, 23 May 1988.
14. Paterson and Webber, 'Federal Republic', p. 144.
15. Murray, 'Ownership', pp. 88ff.
16. Hall, 'Thatcher's Lessons'.
17. B. Jessop, K. Bonnett, S. Bromley, T. Ling, 'Popular Capitalism, Flexible Accumulation and Left Strategy', *New Left Review* No. 165, Sept–Oct 1987, pp. 113ff.
18. Therborn, 'Britain Left Out', p. 125.
19. D. Marquand, 'The Absurdity of a Separate Socialism', *Guardian*, 1 Aug 1988.

Index